move on
without me

move on without me

THE POWER OF A WOMAN
TO CREATE A NEW LIFE
AFTER WIDOWHOOD

Susan C. Beer

 hatherleigh

Hatherleigh Press is committed to preserving and protecting the natural
resources of the Earth. Environmentally responsible and sustainable
practices are embraced within the company's mission statement.

Hatherleigh Press is a member of the Publishers Earth Alliance,
committed to preserving and protecting the natural resources of the
planet while developing a sustainable business model for the book
publishing industry.

Library of Congress Cataloging-in-Publication Data

Beer, Susan.
  Move on without me / [Susan Beer].
    p. cm.
  ISBN 978-1-57826-336-3 (pbk. : alk. paper)
  1. Grief. 2. Widowhood—Psychological aspects. 3. Bereavement—
Psychological aspects. 4. Death—Psychological aspects. I. Title.

  BF575.G7B44 2010
  155.9'37—dc22
  2010006799

All Hatherleigh Press titles are available for bulk purchase, special
promotions, and premiums. For information on reselling and special
purchase opportunities, call 1-800-733-3000 and ask for the Special
Sales Manager.

Design by DC Designs
Brattleboro, Verrmont

www.hatherleighpress.com

10 9 8 7 6 5 4 3 2 1
Printed in the United States

Praise for *Move on Without Me*

This remarkably caring and generous couple have written words of praise which have truly touched my heart. As an introduction to *Move on Without Me*, I would like to share their thoughts with you.

I read your book. It would be too glib to say "I enjoyed it, liked it, it was a good read." None of those expressions apply. It's a thought-provoking "letter" from a woman who shares her pain and passion for re-building her life (her *"re-naissance"*) with tremendous self-determination, motivation, and love of her husband and friends.

It's passionate—in anger, sadness, and love. It's a sharing that cannot help but impact most women—whether they have experienced widowhood, or not. Single or alone, at some point in our lives, we each have to address the feelings of loneliness or being alone . . . and these feelings are inevitably magnified when we lose a lifetime partner.

There's a huge difference between a sense of loneliness and being alone. I have a graphic in my home of an ocean and a pebbly beach. The statement on the graphic is "Do not imagine me to be lonely. Only alone." I remember David was initially saddened that I was drawn to this but then realized it spoke, to me, of strength and dignity, and not the opposite!

Your book has a similar impact. It's very special, and a genuine keeper.

Anne Yeadon
Executive Director and Founder, AWARE USA

A life-affirming, moving and never maudlin blog-styled book. Philosophical underpinnings of Dale Carnegie, *The Secret*, the Bible, "Angelic" support, and positive memories of Andrew ring true without trying to match Joan Didion's metaphysical complexities in her book, *The Year of Magical Thinking*.

David Yeadon
Best Selling Author, *National Geographic Guide to the World's Secret Places*

Dedicated

to

my husband,

Andrew,

with thanks for his love,

for the kind, gentle and good man he was

and

for his encouragement after passing

to

"Move on Without Me"

Contents

The Beginning & the End

The Stage

Winter

Spring

Summer

Autumn

The Closing

Message from Andrew, My Husband

Hello Susan,

I want you to know how much I admire you for your strength to share your beautiful message with all of us. Your mission will touch so many on this earth and your journey from survival to strength will help more souls than you could ever imagine. God bless you for all that you do for so many.

I also want to share with you a *message from Andrew.* He's saying "who would have ever known that our paths/mission together in life would have been the strongest at my passing? Now the world will know your love, your strength and your ability, Susan. I love you."

Keep up your wonderful work!

Trudy Griswold
Best Selling Author, *Angelspeake:*
How to Talk with Your Angels

Acknowledgments

THIS BOOK HAS BEEN made possible through the encouragement and assistance of many individuals to whom I would like to extend my most sincere appreciation and gratitude.

To Spencer Biddle Millius whose spiritual communication from Andrew shortly after his passing empowered me to move forward with my life and to do so positively. His words—*"I want to be with you but I can't. Move on without me"*—provided not only the title for this book but the raison d'être for it and for me personally. Words alone cannot express what my heart feels. Thank you and beyond.

To Balbir Mathur, Founder and President of Trees for Life, Inc., with whom I shared my very first writings two days after Andrew's passing. A dear friend to us both, you came immediately from Wichita, Kansas to be with me and offer your loving assistance. Your encouragement and understanding of me and my writing was the original impetus behind *Move on Without Me*. My sincerest thank you for being a part of it from the beginning and for writing the Preface. You know me well—as a wife to Andrew, as a daughter to my parents, as a friend, and as a creator of linkages.

To Niki Armacost, a dear friend and co-founder of Arc Finance, who said to me "when you are ready, I have a publisher for you." You did and I do. Also, to you, your husband, Tim, and your two sons, my sincerest thank you for sharing your wonderful dog, Pepper, with Monty and me. Monty says "wuf!"

To Loreto Bard, my sister by choice, who took me shopping for new make-up, to make me feel good about me, and for your support and understanding from day one. You gave from your heart. My sincerest thank you and my love.

To Christine Mortimer Biddle, a new friend and very special, what would I have done without you. You accompanied me to the hospital when Andrew passed, to the veterinarians when Star passed, and to the Emergency Room when Monty had a seizure. You were always there . . . then and now. Thank you.

To Henry Bismuth, your friendship was a gift to me when I needed it most and continues so now. Thank you for being the special human being you are, for taking the photos for *Move on Without Me*, for your encouragement to "keep on writing," and for sharing with me your passion for the world of art and for knowledge. And, I mean it . . . all!

To June Eding, my editor, for understanding me and "getting it" immediately. You were amazing. Thank you so much.

To Andrew Flach, my publisher, for taking on a complete novice and understanding from whence I came. Your belief in me and my writing made it all so easy. My sincerest thank you.

To Norma and Dick Flender, Monty's "goddies" (that's short for dog godparents!) and our very good and helpful friends, thank you for taking care of Monty for me when we're in the City. He loves being with you. He bounds in your building and up the elevator, his tail wagging non-stop! He knows he is home.

To Trudy Griswold, you are an angelic presence in so many of our lives, sharing your know-how, teaching us how to communicate with our angels. How can one say thank you for such a sensational gift?

To Memphis Holland, my marvelous friend, for your words of "Grace." They were amazing and so are you. Words cannot express my gratitude.

To Megan and Vic Kaminsky, you gave a total stranger the desk of her dreams only asking that when she needed it no longer, she gift it to another. Your promise and mine, too. Thank you most sincerely for your generosity of heart and spirit.

To Yue-Sai Kan, our old and dear friend, you so graciously opened your home and hosted a party in celebration of his life. I know he was there cheering us on. You were wonderful and beyond. My heartfelt gratitude.

To Leigh, my copy editor, your note was remarkable. We've never met and I don't even know your last name, but you took the time to share your feelings, to write to me that *Move on Without Me* "was so vivid and meaningful to me. I'm glad I was able to be a small part of this special book!" I am very glad you were, too. Thank you so much.

To Cathy Cash Spellman, my extraordinary long-time friend and his, too, for referring to me as an ". . . indomitable force that keeps on going in the face of the odds, and I admire that very much . . ." brought tears to my eyes. Your generosity of spirit in contributing a quote for the cover of *Move on Without Me* exemplifies true friendship and giving to another. How can I ever say thank you?

To Anne & David Yeadon, my new friends, you didn't hesitate a minute when I said "what do you think? Comments, please." Your input and guidance have been invaluable, as to your moving words of praise. My sincerest thank you to two very special human beings.

To my close friends who came immediately to be with me upon his passing—Kate Foster, Mary Morgan Moss, Sahra Lese, Lorraine Vidal, Thouria and Ramdane Benferhat, and Bob Ritch and Riochi Saito—thank you so very much. You were there for me when I needed you most.

And, beyond these very special people, my sincerest gratitude is extended to those teachers from whom I have learned so much over the years. To Dr. Norman Vincent Peale, who wrote with his wife *The Power of Positive Thinking*. For me, you began it all.

xx   *Acknowledgments*

To Louise Hays, who wrote in *You Can Heal Your Life* that "the thoughts we think and the words we speak create our experiences." To Rhonda Byrne, who has shared with us her book, *The Secret*, and the teachings of many Masters. I listen to your inspirational tapes whenever I drive. Finally, to Ron Hall, an international art dealer who followed his wife's dream and upon her passing wrote *Same Kind of Different as Me*. Debbie's story and yours has been an inspiration to me. How fortunate we are to have the writings of all these incredible individuals.

Author's Note

I HAVE BEEN TRYING to think of both an "acceptable" and an appropriate word to describe how this year began. There is only one word that truly comes to mind. It may seem extreme but it's the truth, the way it was. That word is . . . "hell." I might add "on wheels" to express its on-going nature. It continued for quite a while as I am sure you can imagine.

Move on Without Me has enabled me to go beyond the "hell," to emerge from my shell, to reassess and re-evaluate my life and move forward to my new "I am." I trust you will find it evidence that I have succeeded.

Move on Without Me begins aggressively and ends much more gently. You will notice the change, the evolution in my punctuation and grammar! It reflects my own progression and understanding with a little bit—maybe more than a bit!—of revolution thrown in.

My thoughts are not written in stone. They are fluid and adaptable, flexible according to me, you, the time. Please take what you need. If it doesn't fit exactly, feel free to custom tailor it to your own needs and situation. I have. Remember, it doesn't have to be couture, just fit.

This is your future and your time for you just as it was and is for me. It must be. There really is no other choice. Maybe you have children. If so, how very fortunate you are. We did not. I like to believe that if we had, we would be there for each other now.

Move on Without Me has been written from the female perspective. I am a widow. I may not fully comprehend what you gentlemen, what others are going through, although I believe the feeling, the loss is universal, without gender. There is just not the same connotation to the designation widower as there is to that of widow. May I ask, please, that you read this with that understanding and recognize we have all been and are in the same boat.

You might be wondering how my first year ended. My answer, both unexpectedly and most appreciatively, is with grace and wonder. It's all about the power of positive thinking and moving on.

My thoughts and my prayers are with each one of you as you read *Move on Without Me*. There is a better tomorrow ahead.

Preface

I DON'T NORMALLY FREQUENT clubs, and certainly not the Metropolitan Club in New York City. I had gone there for breakfast because a good friend of mine invited me to meet a lady whom he called "the best networker in America."

Mrs. Andrew Beer made her vivacious entrance in her uniquely grand style and joined my friend and me for a very amiable breakfast. Mrs. Beer extended an invitation to me to meet her husband, Andrew, that evening at their Sutton Place apartment. At the time, I was unaware that it was one of the most prestigious addresses in New York City.

Andrew was a tall, lanky, and remarkably handsome man who exhibited excellent social graces. He was educated in engineering at Princeton and business at Columbia and could converse on a wide range of subjects with great ease. That evening started a long and lasting friendship, and Mrs. Beer quickly became "Susan" and then my "little sister."

My wife, Treva, and I stayed with the Beers whenever we were in New York, and they visited us in Wichita, Kansas. During fifteen years, I saw Susan in brilliant action. She knew "practically everyone" in New York City, and if she did not know them, she knew who *would* know them. She was constantly linking people—donors with non-profits, non-profits with projects, foreign emissaries with each other and with influential people in the United States. If someone was going to a foreign country, Susan was the person to call; she invariably found a connection. There were hundreds of people from all walks of life who owed her a favor and were willing to do practically anything for her. Since this was not her profession but rather her avocation, she worked ceaselessly.

Susan Beer was also well known for her social gatherings, especially her dinners. The best of international cuisine was served in grand style. The dining table, extended with two large leaves, could hold a small army. Seated around the table would be a gathering of ambassadors, heads of corporations, financial wizards, intellectuals, authors, entertainers, and representatives of non-profit organizations. After a long multicourse dinner, Andrew would invariably end the evening by offering a toast to the hostess, followed by toasts from several guests.

But life is a pattern woven in the weft and warp of joys and sorrows. Life took a turn for the worse for the Beers. Hit with three financial tsunamis, one after the other, the Beers sold their apartment and ultimately ended up in a modest house in the country.

With great dignity they took all of it on the chin and adjusted to their new life, miles away from the hustle and bustle of New York. Elegant parties at their home were replaced with intimate meals with friends. Susan made sure the meals were delicious and there was always a piece of chocolate on the guest's pillow at night. For Susan, fate had another surprise in store. Andrew died unexpectedly.

When fate takes us in a dark alley, time grinds on very slowly, nearly coming to a halt. But when each moment seems an eternity, we also tend to get clarity about who we are.

Determined and defiant, Susan declared that she was going to carve out a new life for herself; and she would not look back with regret. For Susan, that is how Andrew would have liked it. I can attest to her steel determination because I was there with her soon after Andrew's death.

In her book, Susan has chosen not to give a picture of her

past life and has not included the twists and turns of her fortunes. She did not want to look back, choosing to move forward instead. Admiring and respecting her wishes, I have provided this background so that you, the reader, can get a deeper insight when you read her book.

This is a journal of Susan's first year as a widow. She describes how she had to arm herself daily to meet the tide of emotions that engulfed her. She had to keep her head above the water and pretend to be strong when she was weak. She had to act as if she were lecturing others while she was really talking to herself. As a recent widow, she fights the idea of widowhood itself. Even though she was Mrs. Andrew Beer, she was also Susan, who had her own identity, based on her strengths, gifts, and talents.

But in all those struggles, she is not a New York socialite seeking the limelight or the victim seeking sympathy. She could be one of many women in the world who grieve for their husbands yet try to forge a new persona with whatever lies within them.

That is why this book is of special value to those who have either faced or are going through a similar experience. And that is precisely the reason why I told Susan I should not write this preface. Being a male, I cannot truly empathize with a woman's loss; and sympathy is not enough.

She wanted me to write this piece because she knows of my respect for womanhood itself. I have been a witness to the strength and steel-like courage of women in my own family, as well as the women who I serve in the developing countries.

This is one more story of the steel being forged.

Balbir Mathur

Born in India in 1935, Balbir Mathur came to the United States in 1958 and became an international management consultant. Then a crippling illness culminating in a visionary experience sparked a transformation, and he dedicated his life to empowering the poorest of the poor. His efforts grew into a worldwide movement called Trees for Life (www.treesforlife.org).

This was Him

Andrew, My Husband

J UST SO YOU KNOW. . .

He was six foot three and three-quarter inches tall with brown hair only very slightly tinged with gray. He was in excellent physical shape with the best legs you can imagine. One shoulder was slightly lower than the other due to years of carrying a school satchel too full of books. His brown eyes were deep set and he wore glasses. He looked fantastic in a suit and still could wear the same white tie and tails he wore in his early twenties. He was disciplined and ate everything in moderation. I was very envious: no matter what he ate he never gained a pound. He never smoked and only drank wine to give a toast. He never touched hard liquor.

"Getting lucky" was one of his favorite sayings. He believed in it and the shoe fit. He exalted in celebration of our life together. He loved me passionately. He enjoyed our friends and enjoyed sharing time with them and our extended family. He loved our dogs.

He was an entrepreneur at heart . . . always considering new business opportunities, always exploring new ideas, and, yes, always working. Although he had corporate offices and staff, he kept an office in our home, so work was never far away, including on weekends. I admit, this was frustrating and annoying. He was like a doctor, always on call!

He was truly gifted. He wrote his first book at the age of eleven. It was the story of a famous pirate captain and his horde. Local rumor has it that the treasure was all hidden in a deep and murky swamp in Sea Cliff on Long Island, the town where he lived as a child. Maybe it was and maybe it still is! When his manuscript was accepted for publication by a major publishing house, he turned them down. He felt he was too young. I have it to this day.

He was considerate of others. A gentleman, he always stood for a lady and never forgot a name or a person.

He never hesitated to help another. He often gave too much, or so I thought. People borrowed and never returned the money he loaned them. Thousands upon thousands of dollars!

He wasn't an onlooker. The pathway around the reservoir in Central Park was his favorite place to jog. He was a jogger most of his life. One afternoon, he saw a woman mugged. He gave chase to the culprit and called on his fellow joggers to "catch that man." They did, and the Mayor awarded him a certificate of honor for his part. Although he was proud and thankful and understood the significance of citizen participation, another part of him was sad. He had done his best but not soon enough to prevent her death. The woman died from her stab wounds.

He enjoyed sharing what he read and studied, although he often verbalized like an academician. He would have been a great teacher. He was mesmerized by the origins of mankind. As an undergraduate at Princeton University, he had read his way through their library. Many of the books he perused had never been opened before. He used his trusty red pen knife to cut apart the pages.

It wasn't all roses, our life together. We argued. We made up. If I asked him to do something, it was often "no, I am busy. Maybe later." Later it was and it is now. That honeymoon he was always promising never happened and now never will.

So did I get lucky? Yes! I did. He was a good and kind man and loved me dearly. He was always there encouraging me on, as he did at his passing. His words to *"move on without me"* were his ultimate gift.

That said, he did work too much and loan too much! But that was him.

And to rephrase the words in *Evita*—the truth is, he has never left me.

The Beginning
& the End

Move on Without Me

I WANT TO BE *with you but I can't. Move on without me."* These heartfelt words were my husband's final gift to me. His spiritual presence was felt by the twenty-two year old son of a new friend minutes after his passing. As with his Mother who accompanied me to the hospital, I am eternally grateful.

With his words, strictures were withdrawn. My course was forever altered as he knew it would be. He opened the door for me to focus, when I was ready, on my future. He eased the way for me to go forward and live my life to the fullest and to hold and celebrate his. He did not want me to mourn. "Woe is me" was not my style, nor his. He was a kind and gentle man, considerate and thoughtful to the end.

The Stage

1

The Worst Day of My Life

M Y DAY HAD BEGUN like any other that "final" cold winter's week. I was at home. He was in the hospital. He had been there for five days. This was the sixth. I walked our dogs. I prepared their breakfast and then my own. We all ate. And then I waited.

What could go wrong? His new surgeon had said it would take fifteen minutes, no more. It was a minor procedure to repair a prior surgical error. He had told me, "You don't need to be here. I'll do it early. He'll be back in his room before nine. I'll phone you when it's over."

Minutes and more minutes passed. First, it was nine fifteen, then nine thirty, and, finally, ten fifteen. I phoned my husband's cell and his room over and over again. There was no answer on either number, and there was no call from his doctor. Finally, I dialed the nurses' station. I am told that "He passed at eight forty-seven. We have been trying to reach you. We phoned your cell." He had given them the wrong number. We had no cellular reception at home.

"You waited for me to phone you!?" I screamed and cried at the same time. "You couldn't dial "411" and ask for our home number? It's listed."

I howled in shock and grief. How could this happen? The doctor had said *minor surgery*. Why didn't he phone me? He had all our numbers. They were on my husband's forms. All he had to do was ask his office staff.

Two new friends drove me to the hospital. He was lying in his hospital bed. They hadn't moved him. They had waited for me. He looked the same. His eyes were closed. His mouth slightly open. He had a sinus problem and often slept this way.

I screamed. I cried. I doubled over in pain. I asked why over and over again. I couldn't stop. My friends tried to comfort me. They held me. They said all the right things. Nothing helped.

I kissed him one final time and held his hands. I said good bye and prayed. He was no more, and I needed him so.

We returned to my house. One friend remained with me. The other went to get food. I couldn't eat. My heart felt like it was being eaten alive. I telephoned family and friends. Other friends came to be with me . . . immediately. I was grateful for everyone's presence, but never more alone.

Decisions needed to be made, and only I could make them.

Winter

2

Winter's Reality

WHEN WINTER COMES AND the trees are bare, nature appears silent, stark, and forsaken.

Exactly how I felt! Cold. Stripped. Bare to the bone. Lost. And mad as a hatter! I couldn't get it. Why him? Why me? Why now? Why? Why? Why? Why? I cried. He had so much to live for. *How could you take him?*

The stars shining in the sky, visible through the trees' leafless branches, were just another reminder of winter's reality. Snow's outer crust spoke of its brutality. Icy and white, melting and refreezing . . . just like me. Frozen in time one moment. Admitting my loss another.

Growth was hidden under the snow's icy surface. It masked winter's late berries and branches' new shoots. Frail but in process, just like me. Not accepting. Not yet. But not negating either.

> "Every gardener knows that under the cloak of winter
> lies a miracle . . . a seed waiting to sprout, a bulb
> opening to the light, a bud straining to unfurl. And
> the anticipation nurtures our dream."
> BARBARA WINKLER

3

Decisions

The Most Difficult One

NOTHING BEFORE HAD PREPARED me for this.
What do I do now? What should I do with him? The
first, the immediate, the most important decision.

Medical science had fascinated him. He devoured medical
news. He read all about the latest techniques and discoveries. He
listened ardently to scientific TV programming. He loved it all.

"If I precede you, I want my body donated for medical research,"
I had told him. My Uncle had passed shortly before we were
married and donated his body to the University of Connecticut
Medical School. We had spoken about it then, and he had liked
the idea. So, why not him?

The donation of his body was my decision but his first, as I
learned later.

Later—hours after his passing and my decision to donate
had been made—my godson told me they had discussed body
donation a few months back. It was just a casual conversation
at the time. Scott was sharing some of his medical school and

residency experiences. Although it seems natural now that they would have had such a conversation, the coincidence, the timing, still amazes me. Scott had explained to him how appreciative he and his fellow classmates had been for the generosity of the donors and their families. He felt their donation not only enriched the students' education but helped advance medical research.

Was it the right decision? For both him and me, it was. Absolutely! Although I feared family and friends would be critical of my decision, for it was mine in the end, everyone was supportive. Accord was afforded. I marveled at this.

I could see him smiling, nodding his head, and saying "thank you."

What better could there be, considering the circumstances given? No answer is expected. Just reflect and see if you don't agree.

> "We make a living by what we get,
> we make a life by what we give."
> SIR WINSTON CHURCHILL

4

One Step After Another

Decisions! Decisions!

THAT NIGHT I WALKED our dogs, Star and Monty, up and down our country road. It was late. The sky was ablaze with stars. I didn't want to return indoors. The house felt so empty. He wasn't there. He never would be again.

I had decisions to make.

What about a funeral? Would he prefer a memorial service? Should I place an announcement in *The New York Times?* My best male friend had already done that.

"Star light, star bright . . . Have the wish I wish tonight." I asked for guidance. I called on my angels as I always do. I gave thanks for the years my husband and I had together. I asked why again and again. Part was anger, part was hoped-for answers that didn't crystallize. Instead, there was a reminder of all that remained to be done.

Does this sound familiar? Have you been where I am now?

I returned home and went upstairs to my office. First, I answered e-mails and thanked everyone for their condolences.

Then I did the same with phone calls. Words were shared. What comfort there was, was afforded to both sides—them and me. We each tried. I was in shock. They were doing their best, but how could they know? They were not where I was.

I wanted to deny it. He had looked the same when I saw him at the hospital—although I knew he wasn't. His body, non-breathing, non-responsive to my caress, was evidence he was no longer.

He is in a better place, I was told. *You will meet again,* another said. His passing quickly was a blessing . . . and so on and so forth. I cried and cried within and without. I couldn't stop. I shook. I was oh-so cold. I couldn't help myself.

Then one wonderfully generous old friend asked, "Would you like to have a party for Andrew at my townhouse in Manhattan?" "Yes!" I answered. Not a funeral, not a memorial service, but a party in celebration of him. Perfect. He would love it. A decision made.

This was the way it was. One step after another.

Accompanied by the devastating, overwhelming realization that they were "my" dogs, now. He was no more.

5

Assaulted by Thoughts
& No Sleep
My Writing Begins

THE SECOND NIGHT AFTER and all through the night, no sleep ... again!

Tears lubricated my eyes and streamed down my cheeks. My pillow was saturated! Thoughts came. Some were a direct hit, penetrating: what is to become of "me"? Others scattered like the wind—here, there, and everywhere—leaving a tumultuous wake behind. I was caught betwixt and between: so deeply lost; consumed by grief, by sadness, by anger; and fearful of what was and would be for "me."

I was just beginning to realize how much there was to cope with.

I was alone for the first time in twenty-eight years.

Back and forth, over and over again, I tossed and turned. Thoughts effervesced around me. They assaulted me, demanding to be recorded. Emotionally, I was black and blue. Finally, I switched on my bedside lamp. I picked up my pad and pen—they were always there for noting my nightly thoughts and dreams—and began to write. I sought answers, searching for them and for clues to all my unanswered questions. Morning arrived, and I was still there, writing. As the pages, page after page, flew from my hand, I placed them in a stack beside me on the bed.

Balbir Mathur, my houseguest and long-time friend to both my husband and me, was stirring. I could hear him moving about in his room. He had dropped everything—his own birthday celebration and a houseful of guests included!—and taken the first available flight out of Wichita, Kansas, to be with me.

Over breakfast, Balbir and I skittered from one subject to another. He was deeply concerned for my future. So was I. I was scared stiff! Finally, over chai tea, he asked "How did you sleep?" When I explained my sleeplessness, he asked if I would share what I had written. My handwriting being what it is—illegible—I offered to read it to him.

My new beginning, my new "me," began with my husband's words to *"move on without me."* My transformation began with Balbir's encouragement that morning. Others have contributed since, but this so-generous man, fostered the opening act.

This book is the result.

Balbir stayed with me for four days and, then, returned home to Wichita. Other friends and family came and helped as they could. They had their own families to go home to. It was truly just me and my two black Labrador Retrievers, Star and Monty, and, now, *Move on Without Me.*

6

His Journey Ends

Celebrating Him

I HAD TO ACCEPT that his journey was over.

The party in celebration of him had been sad but incredibly wondrous.

Family and friends came from near and far. It was an evening to be remembered. We toasted him with champagne while feasting on stories and delicious hors d'oeuvres. Brutally cold outdoors, it was warm inside with shared friendships, camaraderie, and joy. We celebrated life—his. Just what he would have wanted.

We shared photos, but, believe you me, they were not worth a thousand words. They were static, frozen in time, whereas our stories brimmed with life. Some I was familiar with, others I had forgotten, and still others I had never heard. Through these, he was brought vibrantly alive.

And, for me, reality was brought home. It struck with full force. I had to accept: I was alone. I was his widow.

A new journey had begun for each of us. He—there. Me—here. I couldn't hide my head under a rock or my pillow and say *no, go away.* There was no one beside me in bed, no one on whose back I could warm my cold feet, no one to say "I love you" or "I love you, too."

The pure love of my dogs helped. Mine slept beside me and kept the bed warm. They touched me and let me know they were there. They got me through the toughest days. People came and went, but my dogs remained . . . always.

You know what I mean. You've been there, just as I have.

But now a new journey had begun. I accepted it because I had no other choice. Actually, there was no choice. It simply is. Life continued on. I was a part of it whether I wanted to be or not. At this point, I wasn't sure that I did.

I had much to digest. Much to come to terms with.

You, too, I am sure.

7

Grieving

The Truth is, I Never Left You

T HE TRUTH IS, I never left you." Remember those words from *Evita*? Madonna sang them with such passion in "Don't Cry for Me, Argentina." I get it. Now, I get them!

He has not left me. I still need his love. I want it. It is there enveloping me—not like a cloud, not always, more like a loving embrace. There is no denying that it surrounds me. And, yes, sometimes it engulfs me, and I feel overwhelmed and so lost.

What should I do? Withdraw my head into my shell like the turtle? I can't get away from it. So, why? What good would it do? I can't hide from reality. Why try? I have to stick my head out and move on without him. He knew that.

He gave me this gift when he said "*I want to be with you, but I can't. Move on without me.*" But was I ready?

Friends gave me many books on widowhood. They thought they would help. Most were real, live, in-my-face depressing. A few were helpful. A very few. The same was true with grieving groups. They rehashed and rehashed. This wasn't grieving. This was submersion. I know what grieving is. I am living it daily . . . that horrifically, gigantically enveloping emotion generated by his passing. I needed to surface.

Have you read *Why Men Love Bitches* by Sherry Argov? A friend gave it to me. Her comment was, "you need this." My first reaction was shock. You must be kidding! What is the matter with you? Don't you get it. Andrew is gone. Then I started to read the book. I howled, and howled in laughter. I needed this. She got Andrew's message. It was maybe a little quirky, but so what. I understood. It felt good.

I am a woman on a new journey. Look beyond my clothing to what I am within. Please! I beg of you, do this. I am evolving. I ask my family and friends not to judge me too harshly but to give me time.

His abrupt passing was not of my choosing. Acceptance was mandatory. The evidence was everywhere. He was not beside me in bed. He was not seated at the head of my dining room table. I couldn't telephone him to say I was en route. *Nada mas.* Nevermore.

There is no black and white in this process. There is only "me." And, you, too!

8

My Journey Begins

Mine Alone

A NEW JOURNEY HAS begun. Mine. Alone.

I have been strong when I had to be. Everyone expected it of me. *Hold up. Keep going. You can do it.* Let the tears come but . . . what about him? All the decisions dictated by what was, by what is, I made. I rose to the occasion. You have, too! There was no choice.

What about me? Don't I count?

What about you? You count, don't you?

There was no time for grieving. There was no time for me. It was all about him. I wallowed in the darkness. I screamed to be heard: look at me; I'm here! People held me in their arms. Mostly, it seemed, for their benefit.

So much required doing. Estate issues appeared and needed to be addressed.

There was only me. Reality had hit hard and fast. I was living it daily. I had to support myself emotionally, financially, physically, and spiritually. Like the tide, the ebb and flow of life continued.

Living differently was a requirement, not a luxury. I had to face my fears, face my new "I am." And accept it!

I needed to think of me. I had suffered the greatest loss, the most horrific. I needed time for me. As obscene as it may sound, it was a luxury demanded. Taking that initiative and allowing myself to grieve and to be angry at him for leaving me was a necessity. Believe me, I was furious. I was deeply wounded. I missed him so. Every little thing reminded me of what had been and was no more, could be no more.

My journey changed every day. There were challenges, and there were gifts. Often each was a bit of both, although some were purely one or the other. I accepted them for what they were and continued on.

You can, too!

9

I am a Widow

No More Pillow Talk

NOT AS TRADITION DICTATES. Times have changed. The luxury of retiring, withdrawing inside my home and from society, doesn't exist. I don't have that option. It's neither viable nor possible. I simply . . . cannot! Besides, it is not a luxury, but an imposition.

"I" am my entire shebang. My future—emotionally, financially, physically, spiritually—is my responsibility. His estate settlement is my responsibility. Our home, now mine, is my responsibility. My living is my responsibility. Everything is "me." Overwhelming sometimes, but there is no other way.

I am a jack-of-all-trades. Soup to nuts! You name it, I do it. I cook. I clean. I change the light bulbs. I shop. I hang my pictures and wash my car. I paint. I walk my dog—an invisible fence would be nice, but not yet! Maybe someday down the road a ways.

I don't till the soil, hoe the fields, feed the cattle and horses, plant a vegetable garden (but I have before), dig wells, put in fencing, or hunt for food, although I know that if had to, I could and would. Nor have I had the privilege of having and raising children. I do wish I had had the pleasure of watching my child take his, or her, first steps, celebrating his first and his twenty-first birthday and all those in between, being there for his graduation from high school and college. It never was and never will be. It is too late.

Landmarks of the "we" have been removed while others have changed. No more pillow talk or lazy Sunday mornings in bed just enjoying and doing what comes naturally, maybe even sharing *The New York Times*! But the bed still needs to be made. The laundry has to be washed and ironed—mine now, not ours. No more him and "me" entertaining friends or enjoying dinner together. But food still needs to be purchased and prepared. The garbage still has to be taken out, and money earned. Responsibilities take precedence.

Grieving has had to accommodate my schedule and circumstances, while traditions have had to accommodate and be responsive both to me and to changing times. There has been no time to sit back and relax, to retire as done traditionally.

I am capable. I have skills. I am socially integrated into the world outside my home—as an employee, employer, volunteer.

This is "me" being a widow. There are things that I miss doing. You know what I am talking about, I am sure! Dancing the Viennese waltz with him. Definitely! Please, add it to the list. I have! Memories embrace me and enhance me. I am grateful for them all. But I still feel so lost.

What about you?

10

Widow-**Hood**

Pray, not Prey . . . Why a Hood

FIRST OF ALL, LET'S get rid of the hood.

It's not the Dark Ages. I am not a nun in a convent covered in a habit from head to toe. Nor am I a bird of prey to be kept from flight. Pray, yes! Prey, no way! Don't worry, ladies; you are safe from attack. Your spouses, too! I pray, not prey! Got it?

Hiding? No! Not that either.

Men are not assigned the role "widowerhood," although the term does exist in *Webster's Dictionary.* (I know. I checked.) So, why "widowhood"? Tell me, please. Explain it to me. I want to understand.

Why are women given the "hood" and men not? It is certainly not a gift. Rather, a weight to behold. Not "to have and to hold," as in the ceremony we all went through with such love in our hearts and such anticipation for the future. We are not wedded anymore. The "we" has been replaced—once again—by the "me." Wedlock is no more. There was no choice.

Women, revolt! Stand up for your rights. The hood imposed

on your head garbs the "I am." It implies withdrawal from the now. We are not there . . . yet. I know I am not! I am alive and kicking and sometimes screaming, "look at me! Look at me!"

If I am to choose a hood, I prefer a raincoat with a removable hood from Searle or maybe Burberry. Fifty-seventh Street, here I come! The choice is mine.

It is yours, too!

11

He is Here . . .
Guarding & Guiding Me
My Guardian Angel

H E I S H E R E. I know it. I feel it. I experience it.

His love embraces me. I see it—visually see it!—every day, every morning when I awake. The branches in that tree outside my bedroom window forming the perfect heart, Paloma Picasso style, tell it all. Tiffany could not do it better. I guarantee it! His message is clear. I get it! I do!

He guards me. He protects me.

He has gifted me with new friends. He knows I will know who and how. There is always a connection and no coincidence. He has also gifted me with answers in unexpected ways. You have probably had this experience, too.

Several years ago, I was introduced to a lady by the name of Trudy Griswold. She and her sister had just written a book entitled *Angelspeake*, which taught one "How to Talk With Your Angels." After taking their seminar, I used the simple little prayer they shared in their book frequently . . . mostly for guidance but often, I admit, for parking spaces . . . and it worked! It still does!

Angel of God, my guardian dear,
To whom God's love commits me here,
Ever this day be at my side
To light and guard, to rule and guide.

Much later, actually years later, I met Megan, the donor of my desk. She told me a very, very interesting story. Every morning upon awakening she said this prayer to protect her nine children. She asked for guidance for the day ahead.

Then, one evening one of her daughters ran out of gas exiting Route 684 and called on her guardian angels. Not the best of locations to be stuck, especially not for a beautiful young girl at midnight. Immediately another car stopped behind her. She was frightened. The driver, a woman in a business suit, got out and offered assistance. She had a can of gasoline in her trunk. What a coincidence! After transferring the gas from can to tank, she returned to her car. When Megan's daughter turned around to thank her, both she and her car had literally disappeared. There was no sign of anyone having been there.

I see him this way: assisting, lighting, and guarding my path. His presence continues . . . differently. The heart outside my bedroom window confirms this. He is guiding and gifting me with people to enhance my life, people to share it with, and opportunities to go forward. Whatever I need comes to me.

His physical presence has ended. His love remains in my heart, my mind, and my soul, as does his spiritual presence. Will this continue? For how long? I can see him smiling his Cheshire cat grin and responding, *forevermore.*

He is my guardian angel.

I see him, feel him with me, and rejoice. If I can do this with my husband, you can do it with yours. You can, too!

12

I Knew I was on the Right Track

My Desk Fit to a "T"

S OMETIMES IT'S AS SIMPLE as a gift telling you this is where you are meant to be. It happened to me.

Megan confirmed it. She came to visit to offer her condolences and said "The fit is perfect." Yes, it is! There is not an inch to spare. My desk is exactly the one I always wanted.

She and her husband gifted it to me the weekend after my husband and I moved here. They were putting it out on the street. I stopped and asked if I could buy it. "No! You can have it. But, when you no longer want it, gift it to another." This was their promise. This is mine.

This gift is no coincidence. I write here, transcribing my night's ramblings. I cry for what was and dream of what will be. *Move on Without Me* began here. Did I know when I saw "my" desk that this would be the way it would be? That from here I would explore who I was, who I am, and where I am going?

This house is no coincidence. His journey ended here, and another began: my new journey as his widow. Megan and I both understood this. It is from here that my new "me" will evolve. Definitely, a better me for all that I have learned and gained from having been married to him and learned since.

To remain or not to remain? The decision has been made. Sometimes it is as simple as the perfect desk. The fit to a "T"!

What do you think? Have you experienced anything similar? If you have, acknowledge it and know that you are on the right track. I have. You can, too!

13

His Estate

Patience & Time

I AM SICK OF it. I am tired of addressing issues. But, I have no choice but to continue on. You don't either. It is part of your financial future, your physical security, just like mine. It is beyond family and friends and personal interactions. It must be addressed.

Memory sustains while estate issues remain. I know! Nothing is completed instantly. There are accountants and lawyers and all that stuff—related and otherwise. It is taking much longer than I anticipated.

One issue after another jumps up. Where is his will? Who has it? Does it have to go to probate? Who are his inheritors? What does his estate consist of? Is it just stocks and bonds? Is your home in joint name with right of survivorship? Were there any other joint assets? Did he own any companies? What about his shareholders and investors? The list goes on and on and on. I know. *Been there, done that.*

There are many things that I don't like that I am having to do. I am doing them to the best of my ability. I am dealing with what comes, what is dictated by law and by humanity. Some issues are resolved instantly. Others that I think should be resolved quickly instead progress by small increments. The reverse is true as well.

I thought one thing was settled, resolved. It wasn't. I wrote the attorney, but I have received no answer. It is a month and counting. Is there no consideration for another? You would think that at a time like this, it would be more evident. Unfortunately, it isn't! Sometimes the treatment received is less than I give my dog. This isn't good, but it is what it is. I am handling it, but I am not liking it.

I am living day by day. Patience, like accommodation, is a trait I am trying to learn. They do not fit my Type A personality: control, immediacy, and instant gratification! But trying I am, with considerable assistance. Dr. Norman Vincent Peale's *The Power of Positive Thinking* has become my lifeline. It reminds me that, to solve a problem, do it in partnership with one more powerful than oneself.

Finally, at my age, I am "getting it"! I call on God, my higher power, and believe. And it's working! Only desperation made me understand its power and take it further. Is this "the Secret"?

My passage through estate issues is just beginning. I look forward to the light at the end of the tunnel when I will be free to focus on me as I need to do. The first time in ever so long. I can't remember when the last time was . . . probably pre-marriage.

If I can handle his estate, then you can handle your husband's. It's not simple. It just is.

If I can do it, you can, too!

14

The Final Straw

Star Passed, Too!

HOW DARE YOU TAKE *Star, too!*

Star, my sweetheart girl, his baby girl, passed exactly one month to the half hour after him. There was no warning. Young and bright and spirited, she was only eight years old.

Full reality struck. Star's passing demanded it. It was cataclysmic, catapulting me beyond woe and woe, poor me, poor me.

How could God or the powers-that-be take her away from me, too? Wasn't it enough he had taken "him"? Guess not; my husband needed Star more than I did. She was the light of my life. When she turned her big chocolate-brown eyes up to me in that "I'm going to do what I want" glance, I knew I was in for trouble. This was her signal.

This was the final straw. It was. I had had it.

Star's passing was the catapult to my transformation. I refused to accept any more. Why her, too? I couldn't understand. I don't understand. Can you answer that simple question, please? Why?

How much more do you think I can take?

I know I have no choice. My anger is helping me. I refuse to give credence to "woe is me" anymore. I will not! I refuse! I miss them, each in different ways, period.

Monty and I remain. I am grateful for him. I just wish they— my husband and Star—were each here with me now. I know. I know. They are not. Or maybe they are, just in another form. I want to believe this.

I am in revolt. No more.

If I can do it, you can, too!

15

My Reality

I AM A WIDOW. I am single. My husband has passed.

I am "one." I was one pre-marriage. I was one, an individual part of the *we*, during marriage. I am one now.

I am alone. This shall not pass. There is no one on his side of the bed. There is no one to fill his seat at the head of my dining room table.

I have friends. They are there when I need them, when I invite them in. They wait to be asked. I am doing this increasingly. They didn't want to intrude until I was ready.

I am resolving his estate- and business-related issues. As I do so, I see myself becoming stronger and know that he knew I could and would cope with all put before me.

I am holding close the past. He was a magnificent gift who enhanced my life immeasurably. I am cherishing the positive and gaining understanding from the remaining.

I am living one day at a time, going forward as best I can. I cannot stop. I have no choice. I am here. He is not.

I am learning that time does not stop for anyone. That I must carry on. No one will do it for me.

I am learning that time and patience with myself, with others, and with my circumstances are crucial ingredients to my journey forward.

I am learning and exploring who I am and where I want to be, recognizing that it will come, though not necessarily when and how I anticipate.

I feel increasingly that this home where we moved prior to his passing is where I am physically meant to be residing now. Originally, I felt we moved here for him, and we did to some extent. Now I know it was really for me.

I grow every day in my understanding and acceptance. He had an inner knowing that I would be alright and that he could depart. It was his time, and it was mine.

My acceptance of my reality has come gradually . . . and with it understanding. My journey along this path is the beginning of my new "me." I am in my infancy stage, progressing to childhood, and with it I have a greater understanding of me and others, as well as my limitations and possibilities.

I have learned to forgive. I was not always perfect, nor was he. As Paul Boese, a Dutch botanist known for his spiritual quotes, said, "Forgiveness does not change the past, but it does enlarge the future."

I am on the right track, with a considerable way to travel still, but with a better tomorrow ahead.

Spring

16

Spring's Awakening

S PRING HAS ARRIVED.

The heart formed by tree limbs outside my bedroom window has begun to awaken from winter's cold. Buds are appearing slowly on its bare branches. Spring's rain, like teardrops, is soothing and nourishing it.

It is the season of growth, nurturing, renewal, and regeneration. I, too, have begun to heal.

I am coming out of my shell, taking a look around . . . just like the turtle. Is it safe? How do I feel now? Can I cope? Progress is slow and increasingly steady.

My long winter's sleep has ended. Just like my heart, which has spent its winter hibernating, I am awakening. Healing has begun. I am taking in nourishment once again.

Remembrances come. My loss, once acute and vivid, is now less so. I relive and replay our favorite times together, sometimes slowly, other times on fast forward or equally fast reverse. Our happiest moments are resurfacing, not as losses, but as times wonderfully shared. It's a magical feeling . . . being alive.

Magnificent green leaves are unfolding on my heart. It is springing back to life. Marvelous how nature takes care of its own, isn't it? And, then, I reflect . . . is that me? Could it be? Do I want it to be? All the questions but only one answer . . . moving on.

If I can, you can, too!

Remember: I am alive and starting to kick or I wouldn't be writing this, and if you weren't, too, you wouldn't be reading it.

17

Walking My Line
One Step after Another

I MAY NOT BE "Walk(ing) the line" as Johnny Cash sang, but I am walking *my* line, one step after another.

Monty and I take long walks in the late afternoon along the quiet dirt roadways around our home. We often bring one of his three friends with us—none can replace Star, his older sister, but each provides the loving doggie companionship that he so craves. This peaceful time surrounded by nature is wonderful for us both. I meditate as we walk, calling on divine guidance and intervention.

There is another walk I walk: my journey on. Memories join me on this. Friends, too, come along.

His estate is in progress. It has generated much turmoil within me and much overwhelming emotion. Some of it has been very difficult for me to handle.

Fear has been my companion, walking by my side. It has many faces. It permeates me sometimes. The fear of being alone. The fear for all that I have to do. Can I do it? The fear for my future.

I have been thinking about this more and more. Where am I now?

18

Mount Vesuvius Erupts

Dump Day

WHAT A DAY! AND, the repercussions . . . ugh! I wish I could rewind or fast forward. Unfortunately, NO! We're talking real time here, not something on your CD player or your VCR.

Stewing and brewing, they finally boiled over. My pent-up emotions erupted like Mt. Vesuvius. What a force! They covered quite a span. It was raining cats and dogs that day. The rain drops persistently tapping on my head should have warned me to cool down. Obviously, I didn't.

It was much to do about his passing . . . more to do with life in general. I had had it. I was fed up.

I was furious at him—how dare he leave me. From perfect health to death in one month's time. His estate was in chaos. I hunted and I sought . . . only it wasn't the game children played. This was life, now! Jane Brody's advice to be prepared and organized came too late. (She writes the Personal Health column in the Science Section of the Tuesday *New York Times*.)

And, people . . . family and friends. That was another ball of wax. Real sticky! I was mad at them, too! Where were they when I needed them most? Why didn't they get it, at least try? I tried to explain my reality. Not "woe is me" but real, live, daily living. They knew he had passed. They knew I was having a difficult time —believe me, "difficult" is an understatement. Where were they? Good intentions, probably, but poor follow through. This hurt. Promise to call? Call. Make a date? Keep it. I understand being busy. I am, too! But excuses—no!

Who paid for my Mt. Vesuvius? The people who were there for me. I was horrific, out of control, and they told me so. I was thankful for that. It showed they truly cared and wanted to help me.

As one friend who accompanied me to my town's charity "Dump Day" that morning said, "the name fits." I really dumped on him. He reminds me of it still. He got the brunt of my meltdown. He was there.

Who else paid? Me! Big time! Stripped bare to the bone and in the dog house! My needs had to be addressed by me. I learned that. Or those destructive, defensive, protective, fear-based, and hurtful emotions would arise again . . . and maybe stronger.

Why did they erupt that day? The lawyers had lost his will. A shipment of school books was lost in Africa. Both were circumstances beyond my control. Either could have caused my eruption. It would have just taken one.

I have apologized. Tears came to my eyes and streamed down my cheeks as I spoke to one and then another. They each said they understood. Did they? I hope so. I believe so. They are there for me still.

My meltdown has made me acknowledge that I am only human. I am vulnerable. My emotional health is tender. It will be for some time. This is all part of my grieving and my living post him.

I am going forward. You can, too!

19

Surfacing, Taking a Deep Breath

Digesting & Forgiving

WHEN I WAS FOUR years old, my Uncle threw me off our dock into water many feet over my head. The tide was high and the water DEEP. I was absolutely terrified. I still, today, remember my panic as I frantically doggie paddled my way to the surface, gasping for air as I finally broke through. Learning the breast stroke took a few more days. My Mother was there to teach me. She had been an Olympic-class swimmer and diver.

Sink or swim? Submersion felt the same now. Instantaneous! There was no preparation either personally or legally.

His loss, his passing, dragged me down. I began thrashing and scrabbling my way upwards and then, finally, to surface. Breathing in fresh air was such a relief. I drew in breath after breath. It felt so good. But I needed more time before swimming forth. The challenge was greater.

What am I saying? I've been sunk in woe is me, poor me, what do I do, what's next, what about me, help me, please. And now

I've begun. I'm ascending out of the depths of my grief. I'm beginning to resuscitate. I am beginning to feel that I can make it. What choice do I have? It's sink or swim. I know it. You know it, too!

What's contributing? Time is one factor. I am digesting my loss. I am acknowledging my fear of being alone and of all that requires doing. I am awakening. I am acknowledging that my life continues. I am forgiving him for passing. I am forgiving myself for not being there with him those final moments. Doctors and nurses were present, but not me, his wife. I am dealing with his estate, his issues. One by one, but slowly, they are abating. I am becoming less frantic, more calm. While not at peace, I can see it approaching ahead. Distant still, but ahead.

What else is contributing? Lessons learned as a child. When I would fall off my horse at riding school, my Mother would tell me to get back on and ride. Quitting was not an option, courage in the face of adversity was. Believe me, I fell off a lot.

I have taken a realistic look at myself. One close friend reminds me to do this every time we speak! Where do I see myself six months from now? A year from now? What do I want? I am encouraged to remember that it is my life and my future now. It is me that counts.

If I can do it, you can, too!

20

Hatching

Get Up! Get Dressed! Get Out!

THE TURTLE HATCHLING HAS broken its shell and emerged. Its journey across the sand to the water beyond has begun. Its steps are slow and a bit wobbly. Tentative, too. This is its most vulnerable time.

Mine too. I have shed my skin. My "we" is no more. I am on my journey forward as a widow, as a single woman once again. Alone, I take my first hesitant steps forward across the great divide between past and present. Memories sustain and support me. I have not forgotten him, but reality speaks! I am one.

On the periphery, friends and family gather. Most offer encouragement, guidance, and support. Ultimately, it is my journey alone. My growth demands it. It is all about "me," about my development, my future. The familiar landmarks of wife and spouse have been removed.

Adaption is the name of the game. Everyone's! Some may assimilate my now while others may not. There is no blame. I understand. For me, there has been no choice. For them, well . . . it simply is as it is.

New people are entering my life, offering their friendship. It's often easier. They know "me," now. There is no adjustment. There is simply acceptance.

Life continues. My sphere is expanding outwards. I am doing. I am handling. I am also aware that ripples remain ahead in both his estate and in my evolution. My path is not without peril. With increasing confidence, I am walking it.

I am sticking my head out and going forth. If there is a concert—I go! If there is a dinner invitation—I go! Whatever it is—I do! *I get up, get dressed, and get out!* I can't sit around and wait . . . he will not walk in the door, take me in his arms, and give me a big hug and a kiss. If wishes could come true . . . how I wish, I wish tonight. But, nevermore.

Instead, I am moving on with my love, my loss, and my memories, as it should be. Tentatively at first, increasingly steady now, step by step, one after the other.

If I can do it, you can, too!

21

Forget Him? Never!

But, What about Me?

FORGET HIM? NEVER!

Friends greeted me at lunch, exclaiming, "You look great!" And, then, "We remember Andrew." That's excellent. I am so glad you do. He was a fine human being. But because I look good, I don't? That was the implication, a very unjust one. Nothing could be further from the truth.

He remains within me, in my heart, my very being. Every day he is in my thoughts and prayers. I am not running away from what was. I am embracing it. It is my reality, as are my memories. But I have to move on. He wanted me to. No other choice exists.

His estate and personal issues have to be resolved. They are my responsibility. Solutions are appearing gradually, but what a quagmire! I told him never to involve me in his businesses. I am now, but trying to be as far distant from them as possible.

Now. Today. It is my future.

"What about me?" I want to scream, rant and rave . . . sometimes. It isn't all about him. I count, too, you know. I am here. Please remember that and remember me.

I know you don't want to hear me cry "woe is me." There is no time for that. No one wants to hear it anymore. Every widow learns that. One week, yes! One month, maybe! Longer, no!

Please understand that I need to move on. Get beyond the sadness ... the sadness that is always popping up and in. I remember him. I miss him. He will always be part of me. But I must live in the now, in and with my new reality. I am alive and I am important, too. So please share your memories, but don't make implications. You don't know where I am. I have not forgotten him.

This is true friendship and love.

If I can do it, you can, too!

22

True Friends

The Gifts of Grace & Makeup

WHAT A WONDERFUL AND powerful gift! A friend just emailed and said that my positive attitude was "grace." To be more specific, she wrote:

> I'm happy to follow your blog—the creativity and necessity of moving forward under all circumstances with a positive attitude is "grace." Having you as a role model for women is uplifting. Not to say some days aren't the pits because sometimes, they feel like it.

She goes on to write about the spirituality of the East and coincidences (if they are that), or, as I often refer to them, simply "magic."

Another dear friend, my sister by choice, took me on a shopping spree for new makeup. We went from one department store cosmetic department to the next until we got the perfect combination of products. She made me feel good about myself.

The time and energy she spent that afternoon focusing on me, Susan, was wonderful. I felt special! She made me feel valuable as a human being again.

It spurred me on to do other things for myself. I purchased new jeans. I had shrunk mine in the washing machine. No amount of weight loss would have helped! My new were truly new . . . hip hugger style! And they looked great! I was changing . . . adjusting . . . adapting.

"What next?" I asked myself. Maybe a new haircut! Maybe just doing things I haven't done in years . . . like riding again. There are horses on the farm where I live.

Friends like these two ladies are invaluable. Their understanding and support is particularly meaningful. They knew my husband. They knew me—then. They know me—now. They have witnessed my transition, my evolution, and, yes!, my growth. They accept me as I am. They are encouraging me to move on by word and by deed.

Being there for someone is the greatest gift possible. Not judging, just accepting and encouraging.

That is what I need now. You, too!

23

Don't Judge Me, Please

My Cartier Watch, His Gift to Me

HIS CARTIER WATCH WAS elegant, classic and refined. He loved it! He wore it every day! I had given it to him as a gift in July, 1998. What should I do with it?

I considered giving it to one of our mutual godchildren. No. They were too young. Styles would be different by the time either was ready to wear it.

Then, a friend who is a jewelry dealer and designer suggested I meet her on Forty-seventh Street in the Diamond District. She had another suggestion.

"Trade it in. Get a watch for yourself," she told me.

Another possibility was to keep it. What for? It would just sit in a drawer.

She took me from dealer to dealer. There was one watch I really loved. It was an octagonal Cartier. It was so perfect. I had a decision to make, a difficult one. Should I go forward? Should I do it?

I finally did make the trade. I wear "my" Cartier watch most every day now. I love it.

There were some comments. "How could I?" they asked. "He wore it every day," they said. They told me I should have kept it as a momento, or, at the very least, given it to a close male friend who would enjoy wearing it because it had been his. This went on and on.

I agree that giving is better than receiving. I have always felt this way and acted accordingly. He always told me that I went overboard. I gave too much. So, don't judge me please, not now. You don't know.

I know that he would applaud my action. He would grin that Cheshire cat grin of his and say that it was about time I gave something to myself. I was entitled to prefer something different, something that was just for me, and, in the end, from him.

You can do this, too. Remember, it is you and he, not others. Listen to your heart. You will know. I did. You can, too!

24

Sticks & Stones

The Impact of Words

PLEASE THINK BEFORE YOU speak.

Words hurt. Understand, please, they impact me and you, too!

One friend said to me recently: "I disliked Andrew." This was right to my face *and* it was in front of others. "He did not treat you well."

Is that true friendship? That's my question.

How did this person know? I like that phrase, "what goes on behind closed doors, remains there." Ours did. Our relationship was known only to us. Our circumstances, too. Our life together was not an open book. Only the cover was seen, and it was well done. He was always a gentleman—kind and good.

The words were unwarranted. They were unkind.

Anyone has the right to dislike another, but is it necessary to say so? Particularly about someone deceased and to their widow? I don't think so. There is appropriateness. And there is inappropriateness. This was not appropriate.

The words stung.

Did I accept that the person meant well? Somewhat! Did I understand why? No! I felt I had to come to his defense, which should not be necessary, not now. He is gone. Why bring up the past, especially your version? It makes no sense.

Be considerate, please. I need real friends. Friends who care. Friends who lift me up, not put me down. If you can't do that, I ask you give consideration and return another day. By then, I hope you will have a better understanding of where I am and what I need, or are simply able to just accept me now as I am.

I give my best with no regrets. You can, too!

25

Friendship, Now . . .

Who's a Keeper?

WHY DO SOME FRIENDS get it and others not?
I have been asking myself this question ad nauseum.

My circumstances have changed. They all know that. They were there at his memorial party. They knew him. They know me and that I have had to adapt. I have had no choice. He is gone.

So why? Am I different? Of course! How could I not be! Maybe not on the outside, although I am maybe the tiniest bit thinner. On the inside, that's a totally different kettle of fish. Turmoil boiled for months.

Am I better? A better person? Who knows! I hope so. I am in process. I definitely am a better person for having been married to him, from having experienced so much since. My understanding has grown.

Do I *feel* better? The answer is yes. Time has worked its magic and I am beginning to heal both mentally and spiritually. Physically, I am the picture of good health.

So, yes! I have changed. But I am also still me. Can't they see that? That is what hurts so much. To lose one's spouse is horrific. To lose one's friends because he passed, I call that abandonment.

What are they afraid of, that I might ask for something? Believe me, I want nothing more than their friendship and kindness. How long does a telephone call take? A minute, perhaps? "Hello. How are you?" You don't even have to say "Let's get together." But, if you do, mean it and take action—set a date, time and place. Otherwise, the words are meaningless.

Am I being overly judgmental? No! Just stating how it is with some, not with all. The majority of my friends are always there. They have busy lives, but never too busy. You know the adage—the busiest people have the most time. It's true. I know from experience! These last few months have taught me a great deal about what it means to be a friend and to be in need.

Friendships have evolved. Some old friends "get" me now and are delighted to be part of my new life. They are happy for me and it shows in word and deed. Others (again, thankfully, few) are running as fast as bunnies with their tails between their legs, so afraid they are going to get caught. Then, there are wonderful new friends who know me as I am now.

So who's a keeper? You tell me and remember *there is a reason and a season*. Friendships don't have to last a lifetime, although how nice that would be. Not all old friends have disappeared into the woodwork. They are few and far between although their loss can have the greater impact. Interestingly, some are returning. This is gratifying, although I ask myself, "why, where were they when . . . ?"

The fear of widowhood is a biggie. Believe me, I know. There is, also, the fear of my dependency and need; the fear of not knowing what to say to me; the fear for one's husband—I'm an attractive, curvaceous widow and available! For the latter, please don't worry. I am not and never will be interested in a married man, or your date.

So what is friendship now? You tell me. But, please, identify yourself first. Are you a keeper? Has your season passed? Are you transitioning with me from winter to spring and on? Is our friendship growing stronger with the seasons?

Remember, I am not judging you, only asking a simple question.

I accept with gratitude your friendship, your love, and your caring, for whatever its length. Ladies, you can, too!

26

Tomorrow…is Just a Day Away

The Sun will Come out

S OMETIMES I NEED INSPIRATION. Yes! Need!
Then, I remember "Tomorrow" and take heart. "It is only a Day Away." The song from the Broadway play, *Annie*, expresses it all. You'll see!

I know the sun will come out. I know my sorrow will lessen. I know I have to face it head on. I know it is a question of time. I know tomorrow is only a day away.

I know the worst is past. My adaption to my new reality and my personal growth forward is the ultimate memorial to my loss.

Remember! What you think, you create. So please put a smile on your face and face your difficulties head on. Say "no more" to pain and sorrow. Say an emphatic YES to joy and happiness.

I am doing it every day, one after the other. You can, too!

Summer

27

Summer's Warmth

S UMMER HAS ARRIVED.
 That heart formed by tree branches outside my bedroom window is lavish with leaves. They have unfolded gloriously. Their green is encasing my heart with vibrant color. Birds are resting on its branches, singing in joy. Summer is here.

The warmth and the intensity of the season are upon us. The branches have received the sustenance for new growth, their memories intact. Just like me.

I have taken my initial steps to tomorrow: slow and steady, just like the turtle. The must-do, the to-dos, once overwhelming, are not so much so any longer. My vulnerability has decreased. With each step, I am stronger.

I can begin to see a future ahead. Not the same one; different. It is sustained and enhanced by what was with him, along with new growth unfolding. Evidence is the new, smaller tree heart taking shape a few scant feet above the other.

Regeneration is underway. Maintenance is next. I must now consider what I need to keep myself hardy inside and out. Early intervention to prevent future problems is a necessity. Have I planted the seeds appropriate to my circumstances? Is my understanding sufficient and correct? Are conditions optimal? Have I done everything possible? Have I both fertilized and watered?

Many, many questions. Only one answer—moving on.

28

Take-off

Ducks are Lining Up

I LOVE HORSES. THEY surround me here on the property where I live. But mucking out their stalls? No! I much prefer the imagery of the TWA ad of several years ago—soaring up, up, and away.

I've been stalled on my pathway more than once recently. My car battery went dead. I had to have both front axles on my car replaced. What a racket they were making thanks to what my service mechanic teasingly referred to as "pothole-itis." I ran out of gas on a dark and dreary night on an even darker, more obscure road in the backwoods of Connecticut far, far from anything. Thank goodness for AAA! These were temporary stalls, easily and immediately addressed. I am sure you have had them, too.

My husband's estate and my new life are another story. I have been dealing with so much. One lawyer took my case and, then, a month later changed his mind and said, "No. It's too complicated." I found another and, basically, the same scenario. They both recommended I jettison his companies. I responded, "No. They are my responsibility. He placed his trust in me." A challenge that I accepted, eventually settling a lawsuit personally without legal assistance. His clients and investors were all pleased with the result. So was I! My husband's accountant presented a very simple solution. Everything was completed in three weeks' time.

There were other issues not so easily addressed. Deadlines that I had to meet where I had no discretion or very little. Then the delays—holidays, vacations, illnesses, other deaths, and excuses galore compounded by people not returning phone calls. One friend had the audacity to tell me that people were not returning my calls because I was needy. It would have been normal if I had been needy after all I had been through, but not here. I explained that I was not the initiator. I was simply responding. The assumption that I was in error was very demoralizing. I preferred no communication to that response.

But ducks were starting to line up. It had taken time. I was resolving one issue after another. Actually, it had been quite interesting. It was only when I had almost finished addressing one issue that the next burst forth to the surface, demanding attention and resolution. Most important for me was that it was happening. At first, it was agonizingly slow. Now, with time and patience, it was speeding up.

Six months prior, I would have been "Sleepless in New York" from all this. Now support and encouragement were leaping at me, just like Monty when he was expecting a carrot or other treat! I was finding viable solutions to difficult problems. The right people were appearing just when I needed them most.

One friend had been particularly amazing. Every time I would feel overwhelmed, he would say to me "keep going, keep on writing." I did.

Like the TWA plane at takeoff, first I taxied in line to the gate and then gathered speed on the ground. I am now starting my ascent. My landing remains in the future. Although I have issues still to resolve, I am in flight and excited by the possibilities and opportunities ahead.

The end of one period of my life has come. A new door is opening. There is no stalling, only an occasional hesitation.

If I can do this, you can, too!

29

Keep on Writing

Three Simple Words

KEEP ON WRITING!

Three simple words of encouragement that have accompanied me on my journey. One friend reiterated them almost daily via voice and e-mail. Others who have read my writings, and some who have shared my journey, reiterated them, too.

My message is simple. It's my story: the story of a woman who has lost her husband. A woman in search of her future, grieving, and then accepting her loss and moving on.

It is also the story of a woman who refuses, adamantly, to be weighed down by the "hood" of widowhood.

I am taking the worst experience possible and transforming it ... and also myself. I am proceeding ahead with a positive attitude. The sun is shining brightly during the day. The stars are emblazing the sky at night. The moon is casting its spell. My tree heart is radiant with new growth. There is a new heart, a smaller one, growing from branches above it. I awake to them every morning, rain or shine.

Yes! I am fortunate in who "I am." I had a wonderful education early on. It has come in handy these last months. I went horseback riding every Saturday morning as a child. I loved to ride although I fell off frequently. I was dragged more times than I want to remember, but I never let go of the reins. As soon as I could, I got right back in the saddle. I am doing that now. I think I have mentioned this before.

As I heard in a dream years ago, "prem ishda." *What I think, I create.* I want to create a sustainable future for myself: one that is fulfilling, rewarding, and, yes!, exciting. Remaining positive and going forward with the attitude that my glass is half-full—definitely not half-empty!—is helping me to do that. My past is a stepping-stone to my desires for tomorrow. They constitute the base for my future and for my writing.

If I can do it, create my new "I am," you can, too! You don't have to write a book. You just have to keep moving on, going forward.

30

Lonely versus Alone

There is a Difference

SOMETIMES I FEEL SO alone. But, am I? Maybe I'm just lonely and using the incorrect word to describe a simple emotion, or should I call it *my need?*

Now, no one shares my home with me but Monty and an occasional invited guest. Basically, physically, it is Monty and me. When we take our walks down the roads adjacent to my home, people wave or stop their cars to ask how I am or just to say "hello." Monty—the pat-aholic he is!—joins in, too! So, although my husband is no longer beside me, there is Monty and there are people around. It is my choice whether I invite them in or not.

My memories also sustain me. I am not alone.

I am lonely for his presence, for another to talk to, to hold, to touch. This was such an integral part of our relationship, and this I miss tremendously.

When you have had someone with you, next to you, and it is no more, the end is always abrupt. The discontinuance of that intimacy is a loss almost akin to the loss of the person. I find myself about to dial him en route home and then remembering . . . no more.

I am lonely. It's only normal. I need. I am sure you do, too! The way to get beyond it is to go forward one step at a time. There have been some reverses, but more and more I am trekking on, steady as she goes!

If I can do it, you can, too!

31

Needy is Normal

Crazed No More

SOMETHING CLICKED INSIDE ME. I finally realized how needy I had been. It came with the realization that I was no longer fantasizing about new relationships. I was not seeking, I was not daydreaming about making love. I was just me . . . again. Thank goodness. What a feeling of relief! What must I have been like before? Crazed, I imagine!

To need is normal. It's nothing to be ashamed of. I was here, he was not. I simply needed someone, something, to hold onto during this most difficult period of my life.

As awareness of my new self began to emerge, the need(s) lessened. I was at the juncture where I could visualize and feel myself unfolding like the leaves on the branches of my tree heart. The colors were incipient but intensifying. It could have been my getting my hair cut that day; as I walked in the main entrance of Elizabeth Arden on Fifth Avenue and toward the elevators in the rear, I was mesmerized anew by its striking, glossy red decor.

I was coming alive again. I saw the vibrancy of colors, and I liked what else I saw: "me." I liked myself, and I could see others seeing it, too. My grin was big. I felt lighter, and, no!, I hadn't lost any weight!

As I was increasingly true to my desires, I came to recognize that they came and went just as people did—some for a reason, others for a season, and maybe some for a lifetime. It was too soon to tell their duration, and, besides, it wasn't necessary. I was under development, in evolutionary mode, and so were they.

So, as I feel needy, I just reflect on the lady who craves a bowl full of pickles and ice cream during her pregnancy. What a combination! The desire didn't last, but it sure caused a lot of scampering about in the interim.

Bottom line—I grant myself permission to need things, people, love, sex. Not everyone or everything requires fruition. Sometimes just the daydream is enough, just the thought. It is all perfect and normal. What a relief!

Been there. Done that. You, too(!!)?

32

TNT,

The Power of a Woman

Turtles & Tigers

W E'RE STRONG. WE'RE BEAUTIFUL. We're passionate. We carry our world on our backs. We're dynamite but more stable. More appropriately, we're TNT.

It came to me in a dream a few years back: *Turtles 'n' Tigers. TNT, The Power of a Woman©*. I have collected turtles since I was a small child, but tigers? This correlation was new. Now I know why it was brought to my attention. My role combines both. So does yours.

It's me. It's you.

Like the world which rides on the back of the turtle in Native American lore, and in Buddhism and Hinduism, my world rides on my back. There has been no choice since my husband's passing. I can feel it, although, like the turtle, I am unable to see it all. Nevertheless, it *is* my responsibility. My progress has been slow, but I am getting there like the slow and steady progress of the turtle in Chinese philosophy.

Our linkage goes further. The turtle's hard and bony shell, which provides protection through nonviolent means, reminds me to have a thick emotional shell, when and as necessary. It represents connection to the earth, my grounding. While molting, shedding pieces of its shell bit by bit, it is vulnerable to attack, just as I have been emotionally as I have journeyed through widowhood. When threatened, many turtle species are able to withdraw their heads, feet, and tails within their shells. I have done the same. I have gone within and come out to make slow and increasingly steady progress just as the turtle does. Like it, I am self-contained. I am "one."

The tiger is another story. It is powerful and strong. You and I are, too. We've had to be for ourselves, for our families, for everyone. I know I am, or I wouldn't be writing this now. We're passionate, sensual, beautiful, and, yes!, ferocious when we have to be. Cruel, too. We protect the family, our cubs. The image of the tiger that is hung outside buildings and houses in China to protect the inhabitants within and ward off evil is a testament to that protective power.

Now, I truly understand. Not dynamite, but the more stable … TNT. The sum total of me. You, too!

33

My First Date

Nothing Made it Easier

I T HAD BEEN MANY years since I last went on a date. I refuse to say exactly—a woman's prerogative—but more than twenty. At the time, it seemed like forever.

I understood intellectually that seeking companionship of the opposite sex was normal. I missed it. It was the way nature made me. I knew, too, that it marked my emergence from the hood and my determination to move forward.

None of that made it any easier.

We met at a play. He telephoned me a few days later and asked me if I would like to join him for drinks. I was both excited and anxious. It wasn't my pre-marriage dinner date when he wore a suit and tie and I wore a dress. This was different. He was different. I was different. We met in the cocktail lounge of a very nice restaurant a few evenings later. I had a glass of iced tea, and he had red wine. He wore jeans and a T-shirt, and I wore black slacks with a lightweight sweater. We talked and talked. He challenged my mind.

I enjoyed his companionship. There were no promises made or given. There were no expectations. We were friends enjoying time together and great conversation. There was no question about what might come next, if it would go anywhere. There was simply a kiss on both cheeks as we parted. I hadn't driven myself into the City that day, I had come in with a friend, so I took the train back home. He went on to a dinner engagement.

This was me emerging from Winter's hibernation and Spring's nurturing. They had provided me the nutrition and the impetus to move on. My mental and emotional clock was ticking.

I knew deep down within me that all would be well— challenging, yes!, but well.

I was moving on without him as he wanted me to do. His final words of encouragement had given me this gift.

If I can do it, you can, too!

34

Dating

Available Men Only, Please

So, I took the dive and had my first date. There have been others since, with other new friends—no one special, just friends.

Although I enjoy men's company, I must say I have not missed the dating ritual. But what choice do I have? None, honestly.

I was introduced to a lady at the United Nations, a deputy ambassador, who had been a widow for eight years. Her husband passed when their son was only five. She had beautiful blonde hair, a great figure, and great dynamism. She had not had a date … yet.

I met another lady, the mother of a friend, who had been widowed four years earlier. She is an older lady but full of life. She takes advanced college courses at the State University of New York and goes out to lunch, dinner, and the theater with her girlfriends, often other widows like herself, but has had no companionship of the opposite sex. When I inquired about it, her response was to ask me if her grandson qualified. So, a great sense of humor, too.

These are dynamic, attractive women just like me. But they have had no dates, no opportunity to dive in—although they are seeking. Men are in demand regardless of status.

I see this as another form of "woe is me," society's imposed woe, which I find quite distressing as it is another weight to carry, and it shows. What has society made a widow into? She is a single woman with needs, no different from any other. She is not a pariah. This isolation of a widow I find absolutely not acceptable.

My personal solution is to go forth believing that "dates" are my right. Any *available* man should be delighted to have my companionship. I am not interested in another's husband, boyfriend, or significant other. I am gorgeous and glorious, and, of course, I smile, smile, smile. For me, there is no other way.

If I can do it, you can, too!

35

There is Nothing Like a Smile
Tall & Handsome on 74th Street

I AM A WITNESS to it. It happened to me.

Remember the song, "When You're Smiling," by Mark Fisher, Joe Goodwin, and Larry Shay, and popularized by Louis Armstrong? Well, the whole world does smile with you. I am living proof of it.

I had just parked my car on Seventy-fourth Street between Park and Lexington Avenues and was about to let Monty out to take him to his "goddies." (Yes, my dog has godparents. I know it's unusual, but it's great for them and for him and me.) I was happy. It was a gloriously sunny day, and I was looking forward to my meetings ahead and dinner with the mother of one of my godchildren. She had just arrived back in New York City. This perfect stranger—a very handsome six-foot-plus, early fiftyish man in jeans with a leather jacket—stopped, looked at me, and said, "Good Morning" and wished me "a wonderful day!" Believe me, the voltage turned up! My smile turned into the biggest grin ever! What a wonderful affirmation of the power of a smile.

One friend, when I told him this story later, asked if I had gotten the man's phone number! Now that I think about it . . . why not?! It's okay. (I'm just kidding. That's not really my style.)

There is power to sadness, too. The opposite kind, but power nonetheless: "When you're cryin', You bring on the rain," just as the lyrics say. Crying! Woe is me! What good are they? What good is this negativity? Certainly, it's not helpful for me or you, or for others. No one wants to hear it after the first couple of weeks. Coddling is out!

But arms open wide when you are positive, just as they did for me.

Friends whom I had not seen in about a year were visiting from Bangkok, which means the last time we were together was before his passing. I was to join them for lunch with three other good friends at the Four Seasons Restaurant on Fifty-second Street. As I approached our table, they saw me and stood up. After we exchanged big hugs, they asked me how I was. When I responded "wonderful," they each in turn stood back, looked closely at me, and said, "Yes, you are." The tone for the entire lunch, which was delicious incidentally, was set by my response. What a difference my smile made. My husband, by telling me to *"move on without me,"* gave me this grace, this gift.

As I am walking down the street now, it doesn't matter if it is Fifth Avenue or Main Street, I smile, smile, smile, and I am receiving what I send out. I am attracting people and things into my life. It is amazing how something so small can have such an impact.

So, I keep those feet a-walking and that smile a-coming.

I am. You can, too!

"We shall never know all the good
that a simple smile can do."
MOTHER TERESA

36

Yesterday, Today, Tomorrow

En Route

WE MOVED TO THE home where I still reside in September. He passed away less than three months later.

He loved it here. Every morning he walked our dogs, and then I gave them their breakfast. They gulped down rapturously their fresh meat (sometimes fish), raw vegetables, non-fat yogurt, and cooked kidney beans and brown rice. You would have thought they were never fed. Believe me, they were and well . . . often better than I fed myself!

We were happy here. Friends came to visit and stay for dinner. Our last Thanksgiving together was here. We had guests from Malaysia. That was my recent yesterday.

Today, I remain here; here in our last home together. It was our final base as a "we." It is my first base as my evolving "me." This book began here, with his passing. He and our life together and "me" were the inspiration, the motivating forces, behind my writing.

"I am" a writer now. "I am" no longer his second. "I am" no longer his sounding board for a new idea he has or a new company he wants to start. "I am" no longer his wife in the physical form. I am my own "I am!" "I am" his "widow," but without the hood.

I am an individual with needs and desires. I play many roles. First and foremost, I am myself. If I don't take care of me, no one else will.

My "me" is a composite of what I want, where I have been, where I was going, where I am, and where I want to go now; as well as what my goals, my aspirations, my learning, and my responsibilities are. All of these make up my entirety.

I am the center of my universe. This was a shock at first. I was so accustomed, after twenty-eight years, of sharing life with another. I knew I had no choice but to accept my new status. Intellectually, I understood. The rest was the problem.

My adjustment is taking time. It and I are in progress. My transformation and understanding of what I want for tomorrow is an evolutionary process. You are evolving, too.

37

Guidance—
That Little Extra Push
The Power of Being Positive

D r. Norman Vincent Peale titled his book *The Power of Positive Thinking*. Rhonda Byrne called her 2006 bestseller *The Secret*. The message in these powerful books, to believe and to be in touch with a higher power, has been my focus, "post-him." These books provided a key ingredient in my development. They provided the sustenance, the way for me to go forward positively.

The power is within me. Intellectually, I get it! But reality speaks. I need more. I admit it. I need that extra push. Help and guidance were essential. Friends were there—some very special friends—and memories, too, but I needed more.

These books provided it. They reminded me of a lesson I learned as a child: that there is something beyond me. Some may call it *God*, others may call it a *higher power*. *Ask. Believe you will receive. Receive and give thanks.* I have and, it has helped.

It's only "me" now. Asking and listening to my inner self and that which is beyond have made this understanding possible. I am no longer a wife. I have Monty and pure unadulterated "dog love." I am not the "me" of pre-marriage or marriage, but a new creation evolving from all that has gone before. These last several months since his passing and our many years of togetherness have changed me forever. I know for the better.

I see opportunity ahead. You can, too!

38

Leaping Gracefully On

Finding My Way

T HERE WAS A MESSAGE in this. I knew it immediately.

A family of four deer came to me in a dream in the wee, wee hours of the morning. They walked beside the road and, then, between two cars. The rest I lost. I had not slept for forty-eight hours and was so exhausted that the hand holding my pen drifted off just as I did.

Then, yesterday, twice, a family of four deer crossed the road in front of me. The first time was in the morning. I was driving home when suddenly a buck appeared, leading his family ever so slowly across the road in front of me. I stopped my car to let them pass. As he advanced, a wary eye upon me, he stopped every so often to glance over his shoulder and make sure I understood not to move, and then he proceeded lithely forward, leading his family.

The second time was about four hours later, with dusk just approaching. I was taking Monty and Pepper (Pepper is my friend's wonderful puppy and Monty's girlfriend and welcome houseguest) for their pre-dinner walk down the dirt road adjacent to my home.

Another family of four deer appeared suddenly from the depths of the woods and watched us approach. They had the most beautiful white coloration on their faces—white circles around their eyes and white beards. When we reached them, and, after gazing at us protractedly, they leapt off *en famille* directly in front of us, with the buck leading. They were absolutely gorgeous and so incredibly graceful.

I was intrigued! I researched their symbolism on the Internet. One site suggested I should see myself as walking in the wood, allowing the deer to lead me into the depths of my soul to limitless treasure within. Another harked back to the symbolism of the deer in China; basically, it symbolizes happiness and good fortune. These are exactly my desires and how I am determined to proceed.

A provocative link! My happiness is coming from within. I can see it unfolding like the leaves on my tree hearts. I am doing more, enjoying life more. There is more inside me than I thought. I am not just the clothes I wear, the image I present. When I complete one thing, I move on with ease and timeliness to the next. I am gracefully leaping from one stage of my life to another, from one situation to the next. Maybe *this* is the connection to the deer's appearance.

As to the number four, I like to believe it is the four seasons through which I am traveling, the first four without him.

Summer is almost over now, a matter of a few days. The last nine months have been incredible. At first, I was overwhelmed by the past and the resolution of issues and, above all, loss. Now, it is me finding my way forward. You can, too!

Autumn

Autumn

A UTUMN IS THE CROWNING glory of the year.
Its blazing colors herald the conclusion of the Earth's cycle. I see this in the ripeness of the leaves on both my "tree hearts." It is interesting how the second heart appeared just above the other; smaller, but equally amazing in its appearance . . . and perhaps more telling. Both are now vivid kaleidoscopes of M & M's®, delicious multi-colorations from fiery red to brilliant gold. They bear eye-catching witness to frost's first appearance and winter's impending arrival.

It is a time of maturity, of conclusion, just as it is of my first year of being a widow.

The leaves are soon to fall. I will rake them and prepare the ground for the year ahead.

My journey from past to present, from what was to what is, from being a part of the "we" to being my own "I am" is much the same.

There is a season for everything. Nature prepares me, as I am now preparing for what is to be, for my new "I am."

40

I Am

Joy—My Middle Name

A T FIRST, MY "I am" was a woman widowed. Overpowered, overwhelmed, sick at heart. It was all about him. It was about all the decisions I had to face, about getting from one day to the next. It was about my survival.

I was unprepared for his passing, for all that happened next and for all that I had to do. I was in shock, in deep despair.

My dog, Star's, passing provided the catapult away from "woe is me." I had to come to terms with reality, and it wasn't good. I was furious and determined to turn my life around, to move on.

The education I received from my parents and my Aunt Gracie provided me the tools to do so. My Mother had been a great athlete and always stressed that it wasn't if you won or lost, but how you played the game that was important. She felt athletics taught one how to handle adversity and defeat without quitting. Gracie stressed strong ethical and moral standards, knowing who you were—the basics.

My extended family, multicultural as they are, encompassing

various religions from Christian to Muslim, Buddhist to Hindu to Jewish, taught me to value the quality of the human being, not the color of their skin or their country of origin. We are all equal. As the Native Americans say, "we are one."

The wonderful people and non-profit organizations I work with have taught me that what is important for my survival, for my transmutation as well as transformation, isn't being provided the fish, but learning how to fish myself. They have taught me to survive and to survive well. I should have remembered this after all the years I have created linkages with Balbir Mathur. He works with the poorest of the poor in developing countries, providing them with the tools to survive, from nutrition to education. Working with people like Balbir, helping the world's neediest, has been my pure joy!

Saying this makes me realize how prescient my parents were when they gave me my middle name, Joy. I haven't used it since I was married. I think it's time I do so again.

Who I am now is a work in progress. I have revolted against "woe is me" and taken my life back into my own hands. I have transformed what was the worst event in my life, his passing, into a pearl.

I am much more now than I was before because of what I have gone through, because of him and all of them.

As expressed in the African word and philosophy *Ubuntu*, I believe, "I am what I am because of who we all are."

You are, too!

41

Regrets

Yes! I am Human

I HAVE MANY REGRETS! I am sure it's the same with you. It's called human nature.

I had arranged for the special advisor on energy to the president of an African country to be a guest speaker at the State University of New York at Stony Brook's Advanced Energy Conference. I had also received invitations for myself and a guest.

I knew my husband would enjoy being there. Instead, I invited a friend. I knew it could be an important conference for her, as she had just co-founded a not-for-profit dedicated to microfinance, renewable and alternative energy, sanitation, and water.

A few short weeks later, he passed.

I deeply regret not taking him.

He would have enjoyed being at the conference, meeting the participants, and just being with me. He would have especially enjoyed meeting the guest speaker. They did speak on the phone at the conclusion of the conference as I was driving him into the City, but they had much more to share.

It is too late now.

I have to accept my regrets and embrace them. I can't eradicate them. Rather than knocking my head against the wall, I treat regrets as opportunities, as examples of something not to repeat. "Been there, done that!"

Sometimes, in my mind, I take his hand and ask him to join me so I can share with him a prior event, one that he was not present at. I have done this with the Energy Conference. I can see him smiling and saying, "Thank you."

It is all a question of my learning from every situation, whatever it may be.

If I can do it, you can, too!

42

Coulda, Shoulda, Woulda

Promises! Promises!

THERE ARE SO MANY.

I wish we had had a honeymoon. He always said, "someday, soon." Promises! Promises! I wish I had taken him with me to the Advanced Energy Conference a year ago. I wish that I had told him I loved him more often. I wish I had made him Schnecken more often, too. He had loved these German honey buns since he was a small child, when his Grandmother made them for him. I wish I had given him that book by Conan that he wanted for Christmas two years ago. I wish that I had not yelled at him. I wish that . . . .

More and more wishes and all too late!

So, why focus on the past? It doesn't help me or him, or you either . . . now!

We each could have done things differently. Maybe we should have. *Maybe. Maybe. Maybe.* My answer—so what! There is no turning back. The only motion is forward. Like nature, season by season, step by step.

This final season, Autumn, is upon me now. Nature's abundance has reached its pinnacle, producing glorious shades of gold, orange, red, and brown. Shortly this, too, will pass in preparation for what appears to be sedentary but is actually the revitalizing phase of Winter. Nature, on the surface, will appear dormant, while underneath, unseen, preparations are underway for the year of growth ahead.

I have learned much this year, from the past and from his passing. I am using that knowledge, those remembrances, that growth, and my experiences now to go forward with my new life. Now and then, I add a little Miracle-Gro®—my own personal, in-house, in-your-face variety learned from my Mother: *Get up, dust yourself off, and try all over again.* The better I fertilize my life, the better it will grow, and the better it will be.

I am not living in "coulda, woulda, shoulda land," but in the present, and moving on. I am doing new things and old, basically whatever it takes to bring joy to my life and lightness to my step. I am going to the theater, watching movies, taking walks with Monty in the country and in Central Park, having lunch and dinner with friends, becoming re-engaged with life and living. I am going to start yoga classes again now, start riding again in the Spring, and, when Summer returns, maybe visit my family abroad.

I am opening my door to possibility. My life has changed in unexpected ways.

If I can do it, you can, too!

43

Holidays, Like Memories, Continue On

Christmas Now

I LOOK AT MY collection of turtles and visualize them continuing on, one stacked upon another. In Native American lore, they support the world just as my memories support me.

Holidays are like this. Remembering brings them back and continues them on. There is joy in knowing that we shared them. There is also sadness that he isn't here to share them with me any longer. He enjoyed them so.

Tradition and celebration were important to us. Sharing our home, especially on holidays, was an integral part of our life together.

Christmas last year was difficult. He had passed just twenty days earlier. I was raw. My eyes were red from crying. I felt overwhelmed. But I knew he would want me to continue on. We had it all planned, both our guest list and the menu. Our gifts were wrapped and ready to put under the tree. Extended family and friends had confirmed their coming. They wanted to support me. They didn't want me to be alone. This was my first holiday without him.

It wasn't the same. There was no way it could be. He wasn't with us. Over lunch, we shared favorite memories of Christmases past, and, with dessert, we toasted him. We celebrated his life and his contribution to ours.

I celebrated the time he and I had together. I celebrated him and "we."

It was a tentative new beginning. Was it too soon? I took my tree down immediately. Does that answer your question? I couldn't face seeing it there. It was another reminder he wasn't here, that I had celebrated my first holiday alone. But I continued on. In the end, I was happy I did. I did it for them, for me, and, yes, for him!

Friends both old and new joined me this Christmas Day. Not the same guests as last year. This was normal, though somewhat sad. Times have changed, and so have I. It was a wonderful day. My tree was beautiful. My fireplace was ablaze. Everyone enjoyed my Christmas menu, especially my dessert—my Christmas cassata was divine! We toasted Christmases past and present. We shared memories. There was joy around me. The spirit of Christmas was here. I knew he was here, too, encouraging me on.

If I can do it, you can, too!

44

Gratitude & Growth

. . . with Abundant Hope

for the Future

I KNOW YOU ARE thinking, "how could she be grateful? Her husband passed away. She is a widow just like me." You're absolutely one-hundred percent correct. I am not—definitely not—grateful for that. I want him here beside me . . . right now! I miss him.

But I am grateful.

At first, when I could finally address it, I was grateful for his sake that he passed quickly, that he didn't suffer. There was no long, protracted illness or incapacity. This would have been hard for him. He was too vital and alive. Later, I was grateful for myself as well. The spouses of so many friends had gone through so much. For both him and me, ultimately, this was a blessing.

I am most grateful for what he was and what he gave me—his love; many, many remembrances; and the encouragement to *"move on without me."*

My gratitude is also for my personal growth. I have grown to understand more about people and how they act and why. I will not treat others as some have treated me since his passing. I will be there for them to the extent they would like me to be.

My capabilities and my skills have increased as I have handled his estate alone. I have dealt with his businesses to everyone's satisfaction. I believe he knew I could handle things for him and that I would handle them—although, if you had asked *me* either before or when he passed, I would have told you it was out of the question, impossible. I have new friends, good ones, in the town where I live. I have written this book, *Move on Without Me*. These are all reasons to be grateful.

The first time I went to a psychic was shortly after I married my husband. Beatrice didn't use a Tarot deck but a regular deck of cards. She did a general reading, predicting I would one day write and also that I would have many godchildren and a close tie to Asia. She was right on all points. This was January 1981. I had learned of Beatrice Rich through an article in *New York Magazine*. She was well known and well regarded. At the time, she did her card readings at a restaurant uptown in the East Eighties. She was amazing. She has since become a friend.

Move on Without Me has made me that writer. It is a direct result of his passing and my life both before and since. It records the good and the bad—I prefer them in this order!—and all that is in between. It is helping me to go forth into my new life without him. It is definitely not the way I wanted to become an author, but it is the way it has happened.

I have learned much since my widowhood, much about me. The buds which appeared in Spring on my tree heart reminded me of Earth's regenerative power. The gorgeous and magnificent green leaves of summer warmed my heart, for I knew that the power was within me, as it is with the Earth, to regenerate myself. I could see the seeds I planted upon his passing blooming into the woman I would become. I saw her unfolding; that seed, after the cold of Winter, emerging as a tiny bud in Spring, and, with Spring's not-so-gentle rain and Summer's warmth, opening into a full and magnificent leaf. The drought was over. With Autumn's end, the cycle will be completed. The leaves, gloriously golden and red now, will fall. A new year will begin.

Growth is natural, mine and nature's. His loving words and this book are on the path with me as I walk from widowhood to my new "I am." This walk is an integral part of my development. I am grateful for it and for the man, my husband, who has made it possible. My love remains with him as I go forward with abundant hope for the future. There is no other way.

This is my way. It can be yours, too. Please allow it. Go with it, if I may!

If I can, you can, too!

45

411: Information, Please

In Your Heart

IT'S MORNING. MY ALARM rings. I wake up and ask the universe for guidance and sometimes for information.

The answers come. They are both timely and correct. Not always what I want to hear or when, but they come. It might be through a person I meet, a thought that pops up, an article in the newspaper that catches my attention, or simply my dog demanding a caress—his undeniable right.

I still ask my whys. So many are still unanswered and probably always will be.

I know he was ready. I know he did not want to leave me. I know he loved me dearly. I know he gave all that he could. I know he knew I would accept his passing . . . eventually. It would take time to move on, but I would do so. He knew I didn't give in or give up. It wasn't his style or mine.

His words—*"move on without me"*—were an exquisite gift of love. They shine brightly within me. They encourage me on to do better and to be more. I carry them and him within me.

There are two tree hearts now outside my bedroom window reminding me, everyday, that he is here. The form is different. The message, the same. *I love you. I am here with you forevermore.*

So, if you will:

"411, please."
"City and state?"
"The Universe, please."
"Yes?"
"What is his address now?"
"Madam, it is in your heart."

Indeed, it is.
That says it all.

46

Forever in My Heart

Never Forgotten

I HAVE NOT FORGOTTEN him or us . . . just moved on as he requested I do. I think about him often, that gentle, caring man who passed, leaving me such a gift of life. He is a part of me and will be always.

He is not forgotten, only in a different place. I envision him surrounded with love from his family, my family, our family, and all the friends who have passed before. I see him and Star, his baby girl and my sweetheart girl, walking side by side, keeping each other company. He is not alone nor am I. I feel him watching over me, encouraging me, and thanking me. His grace is evident here and throughout this book; in the text, the words are gifted from him to me, and shared with you. If not for this gift, there would not be this, now.

Near my home in a village northeast of New York City is a strikingly beautiful stone Episcopal Church, St. Matthew's. It will celebrate its bicentennial in 2010. Every time I enter its doors, I think that "he" would have loved it here.

Recently, the Rector, the Reverend Terence Elsberry, reminded me of my very first visit there. It was the last Sunday in December. I had seen the church many times while driving past and thought how incredibly beautiful it was. I wanted to attend their Christmas pageant—I had seen it mentioned in the local newspaper and on signs in the adjacent area—but a snowstorm intervened. This Sunday, the twenty-third day after his passing and the day of the memorial party celebrating his life, I finally went. I was expecting nothing, but hoping for much. And so it was. Terry's wife had suggested he not preach a sermon that morning, but instead that the congregation should sing Christmas carols, and so we did. Tears streamed down my cheeks as I sang from my heart. I love the spirit of Christmas. But this was a special day, too; his day. I oft times visit there still on a Sunday morning to hear Terry's sermons. They are not lectures as one experiences so often in a church or from a pulpit or podium. They are inspirational talks and the sharing of story with inspirational words that I frequently find myself writing down. I sit beside a window and listen and remember. Sometimes I find myself looking out that window and seeing beyond my husband passed and our life together, all of it as if framed in a painting.

So, you see, he is with me always, just in a different form. My extended family and I have prayed for him at Sufi Zikars, in churches, and in temples. We have meditated and seen him before us saying "thank you" first and then "good-bye." He was always the politest of gentlemen. The venue is immaterial, for I know he knows and is saying keep on, keep on, *"move on without me."* It is time. That is my job now, my responsibility to him and to "me."

And yours, too, to you!

47

Moving On . . .
I Have No Choice!

Everything Ventured,

Everything Gained

I GOT ALONG WITHOUT him before we met, and I have to get along without him now. I have to move on alone. I have no choice.

Our period of togetherness is over. It is not forgotten. It is what sustains me. That and my knowing that in order to survive, I must continue on. I must support myself.

Part of supporting myself is remaining positive. I don't focus on "woe is me." Instead, I feed myself with uplifting thoughts that maintain my mental and emotional health. I teach myself how to "fish." I don't wait for someone to provide me with the fish. I am independent financially, not dependent on another. As I address my life's situation, I am thankful for all that I have, for all that I had, and for all that I will have. I believe that I am entitled to more reasons to give thanks and immediately do so as they appear.

I can do all things through Christ which strengtheneth me. And believe. I adopted these words of advice after reading the works of Dr. Norman Vincent Peale. Every morning before I arise from bed, every time I walk Monty along our dirt roads, every evening before bed when I meditate, I give thanks and believe.

I look with hope to tomorrow. I maintain a positive attitude. Everything ventured, everything gained is my philosophy. I am not perfect, but I am in process. "Under development," if you prefer.

I seek wholeness as a single woman whose husband has passed. My memories, our love, are part of me. My future is ahead of me. It is my challenge and my choice.

If I can move on, you can, too!

48

Year's End

I am Moving On

THE PAINTING OF HIS life is complete.

I have given his clothing to family and friends. They have been most appreciative of having something of his as a wearable remembrance. Other items I have given to people in need. I have offered his family paintings to his niece and nephews. They are married and have children of their own. These are part of their heritage and rightfully theirs. I have put some of our photographs in albums rather than having them all framed and on display. I traded his watch for one for myself: the same make, but a woman's style.

The painting of my life is in process. What began as a clean slate at my birth has much empty space remaining, waiting to be filled. There is much to do before my final sleep.

My goals have changed, as have my fears. What I once would have considered a rejection, I now see as a challenge and an opportunity. What I once would have considered a failure, I now see as a learning experience.

I am moving forward to the very best of my ability. I am tacking with the wind, sometimes trimming my sail, other times luffing, reaching, or jibing, but more often running full-out with sail extended.

I want to be a fully awake, fully contributing human being who is interacting positively with others every day, and in as many ways as possible. I want to make a difference not only in and via my own life, but to the lives of others. This is not ego; it simply is who "I am." I want others in my life and maybe a significant other someday. I continue to release the past and integrate it into my now. I have acknowledged my loss, recognizing that it will always be with me but transposed. I have learned that his love never leaves me but heals me. I am moving forward, aspiring to be all that I can be.

I am moving on. Life has changed, and me with it. My viewpoint has changed. I continue thinking, being, living; but differently. He is no longer here beside me in physical form. He is here in love and memories.

I have accepted the challenges placed before me with ardor. *Move on Without Me* is proof that I have.

You can, too!

49

I am Single.
My Husband has Passed
The Fit is Right

I AM SINGLE WITH a codicil. My husband has passed.

A "codicil" is defined by *Merriam-Webster's Online Dictionary* as "a legal instrument made to modify an earlier will." It is also, more generally, an addition, appendix, or supplement to the original. This is why I prefer to say I am single with a codicil: my husband has passed.

The fit is right. Maybe not for you, but for me. Yes!

The term *widow* is used on applications for bank accounts, credit cards, marriage licenses, vehicle purchases and leases, apartment leases, and home purchases and rentals. The list is exhaustive and strictly legalese.

I am not a legal entity. I am a woman whose husband has passed. A single woman with a codicil. Basically, let's face it, I am one in number, an individual.

"Single," by the same dictionary, is defined as "consisting of only one in number." That's me! As his widow, I am one. Divorced, I would be the same, but with a different codicil.

It is the categorization I object to. The physical fact of being a widow—I have no choice. It is reality. My reality. He has passed.

My life has been enhanced by him. This will not change . . . ever.

Our relationship has changed, and with it my journey. I walk Monty alone now. No more long walks together, holding hands, with our dogs beside us. No more physical attachment. I am single. I was married, but I am no longer. My husband has passed.

So, select the title that fits you. As close "to a T" as you can, please. I have. You can, too!

50

My Year of Reflection

M Y HUSBAND PASSED AWAY a year ago. I thank him for his love, his encouragement, his presence in my life—as he was then and as he is now and will be, forevermore.

I am happy now and more at peace. It is not that he is forgotten, for I miss him every day. It is how I experience his loss that has changed. He is a part of me, and, for this, I offer him my most sincere and loving thank you.

Most people look at the passing of a loved one only in the negative. Once upon a time, I did so as well. Beyond the loss itself, for it is the most devastating, is the fear. The fear of today, of tomorrow, and fear for oneself. Where am I going to be, what am I going to do, who is going to take care of me, when is it going to get better? The four big W's—who, what, when, where—are all fears reflecting *me*, not him.

From the minute I began to understand this and act on it, my life and my journey were transformed. Suddenly, life required my personal action—and perhaps a bit of revolutionary change within.

"I am" a far better person for having been part of our "we." I have no regrets that we were husband and wife. I would have liked more years with him, but they were not to be. Instead, I have learned to deal, to handle, to cope with a myriad of issues and circumstances including, most significantly, being single again.

I have grown into a woman I like. This is due much to him. It is a combination of my past, what we had together, what I was then, and this past year without him. With his passing, I have evolved, as I had to do. I have learned that I was capable of much more.

I am proud of who "I am" now. I have transitioned from the financial community to the writing profession. I still and will always create my "linkages," as they are an integral part of me. They are my joy, beyond my middle name! To make a difference in the lives of the poorest of the poor is a blessing beyond anything else. I have friends, both male and female, around me. I have my godchildren and my wonderful black Labrador Retriever, Monty. He is six years old now.

I have an extraordinary life . . . one for which I am most grateful and appreciative. I look forward to many, many tomorrows, each and every one an enhancement from the one before.

My year of reflection is over, and yet it will continue as an integral part of me as a new and vital life awaits me. "I am" and continue to be evolving. I give thanks to each and every person who has participated and helped me along my journey.

Life is amazing and, truly, a gift to celebrate.

The Closing

You Can Deal
with Loss, Too!
Yes, You Can!

MY LIFE HAS CHANGED. If you are dealing with loss, then so has yours. We are no longer two as one, a "we," nor will we be again.

Remember, today is what counts. How we treat our remembrances, how we acknowledge ourselves, how we interact with others, how we give to ourselves, how we take care of ourselves, in other words, it is all about you and me, the individual "I am." It takes adjustment, it takes time to comprehend the new reality that surrounds you, that is you, but do it you must. Once embraced and as you realign yourself with what is, others will be there to help. If they are not, accept and go forward without them. They may return another day. As for others, some will remain and others will not. What is important is that you are doing and taking care of you. Whoever is there is meant to be whether it be for a day, a month, or a lifetime. What is important is that they were there when you needed them.

Life changes, and you must with it. I have learned this sometimes easily and sometimes the hard way. I have accepted where I am now and who I am now, and I look forward to what I will become, although this is an ever-changing, daily evolution, and sometimes a revolution.

I have learned to let go of the baggage of the past, to accept people for what and who they are and myself as well. I no longer expect excellence from everyone. They have their own "I am" that must be addressed and for which they are responsible. I have learned to give thanks and to mean it.

I have learned to express my feelings, what I need and what I want.

I have learned to express the joy that is in my heart and to share it with others.

I have learned to laugh once again!

I have learned that there is a wonderful tomorrow ahead of me every day, if I allow it.

I have learned to live and to truly enjoy life every day in every way. It is not always easy. There are days of sorrow, of deep wanting of him, and others of "why me," but there is no other way. I look at every challenge now as an opportunity to learn, to grow, and I have and as I will continue to do forevermore.

There is more to me than I thought. My knowledge and my abilities have increased. My understanding of myself and others has increased. My desires have both altered and increased. I have dug deep and emerged to find myself in a period of tremendous self-discovery. I grow more each day.

Move on Without Me has been a gift to me of learning and of acceptance of what is and what will be. It is about passing, about living, about going forward. It has enabled me to accept joy into my heart and to give joy as well. Joy is my middle name.

The power and the desire to move on is within you, as it was within me. If I can do it, you can, too!

Most Sincerely,

Susan

This is Me, Now!

J UST SO YOU KNOW...
First things first ... I am five foot four inches tall with short, light brown hair and blue eyes. I am in excellent health and in good physical shape with a few wrinkles here and there. I am told I have a good figure. I lost a few pounds when he passed and have now regained them. I love desserts first, last and always. I hate diets and dieting. Now you know why I focus on Rhonda Byrne's teaching in *The Secret*—I am the "perfect weight." Let it be so, please! That and no gray hair, thank you very much. Actually, the lack of gray is due to my Mother's great genes, not to a bottle of hair dye—she passed at ninety-one with nary a gray hair on her head. Generally, I try to eat in moderation and act with moderation. But, honestly, it doesn't work. I am "type A."

I serve on the Board of Directors of several not-for-profits, one with my best male friend of twenty-five years and another with one of my closest female friends.

Now, let's move on to the nitty gritty of *NOW*.

I am single. My husband has passed. I have accepted his passing and begun to see other men. There is no one in whom

I am interested but . . . maybe someday. That is for time and circumstances to tell. Not now, not yet.

I have remained in the countryside where my husband and I moved shortly before his passing. The correct addition to that statement would be, "for now." The time will arrive when I will return to Manhattan and the country will become my secondary residence. Not yet, but someday.

I am an author. Beatrice Rich predicted it in 1981. It has taken almost thirty years for "author" to become part of my "I am" but it has, which is most important.

"Me" is creating linkages for the poorest of the poor in developing countries. Working with people like Balbir Mathur, Phil Lane, Jr., Frederique Darragon, Sam Daley-Harris, Professor Yunus, and Niki Armacost, among others, linking them and their not-for-profits with governments, multi-nationals and other not-for-profits for projects involving micro-finance, education, and women's and children's health is an integral part of my "I am" . . . past, present and future. It is my pure joy.

I have firmly and determinedly exited the financial community. This was my husband's interest, not mine—although I was a stock broker when we met and for a number of years remained in the field in an administrative capacity, I am no longer involved today. To say I hated it would be inadequate. It was simply not me. It was him.

I have a couple of college degrees. They are not who I am either, just a part of my background. Their importance has diminished as I have grown older—I am sure you have found this to be the case as well . . . work and life experience take precedence.

I dearly love architecture. I am fascinated with it, with building design. I wish I had studied it in college but, unfortunately, I did not. I wonder how that desire, that love is going to manifest itself now. I know it is going to be an integral part of my next persona. I promise to let you know where it takes me as opportunities present themselves. As a beginning, I am studying art and painting, and working with an extraordinary artist.

I need to work and be productive. I have no choice. Be it art or writing, or most likely both, every day offers a new adventure and a new opportunity. There are still a few issues from the past I am dealing with, basically financial. I have had to accept them in order to be able to resolve and end them. This is the way it is.

It is me moving on as he asked me to do.

It is Susan, now.